In memory of Martin Plaut, my father and teacher

Everything in this book is factual

All events, other than those clearly identified as legend,

did in fact occur

CONTENTS

We scout out the wall like the blind,
and we probe as if we have no eyes,
we stumble at noon as if it is night,
among the strong who are as the dead.

– Isaiah 59, 10

1. The Ambush

SCORPION PASS is still one of the worst roads in the Middle East, a nightmare even today for the best of drivers. It is where the earth suddenly drops down from the plateau of the Negev desert south of Beer Sheba to the arid wastelands of the Arava Desert. The road from the Heights zigs and zags down the face of a cliff until it reaches the plain below. From there, the highway straightens and runs through land so parched that even cactus refuses to grow. It goes all the way to Eilat on the Red Sea, the site of the port from which King Solomon's ships sailed the world to bring riches and wonders to Jerusalem. The Queen of Sheba once disembarked there and made her way over land to Jerusalem, climbing Scorpion Pass along the way.

It was the middle of March in the year 1954. The road through the Pass was already choked with dust during the day, even though the summer was still far off. The thin covering of green that sprouts up over the sands after the winter rains was already dry and brown.

A civilian bus was winding its way back and forth up the face of the mountain, climbing the Pass, headed from Eilat to Tel Aviv. It was late in the afternoon. The desert heat was dying away and breezes blowing.

As it made a turn through one of the tighter twists, the bus was raked with gunfire. The driver was killed instantly. As he slumped over the steering wheel, his arm jerked it to the right. The bus slammed into the wall of the mountain on the side of the road and halted, with its front jammed into the hard dirt. Had the bus instead lurched to the left, as the shooters had intended, the bus would have gone over the precipice.

Six men fired into the bus. When the screams stopped, two of them entered the bus and walked up and down the isle, firing into the bodies to finish them off. When they had completed their work, there were eleven people dead, including the driver, the driver's wife and his son. Three others, including the driver's daughter, were still alive but left for dead, covered with their own blood and that of the others. The killers then slowly worked their way through the bus a second time. They took the guns from the bodies of soldiers who had been heading home on leave. They went through the bags of the dead, looking for valuables. Finally, they left.

In a region known for its violent horrors and terrorist atrocities, it was the worst massacre since the end of the War of Independence and the worst the country would know until 1970. The massacre was more than a "mere" outrage. For years Israel had been experiencing random murders, shootings, bombings from infiltrators. This however was something different. It was the catalyst for a diplomatic crisis and it threatened to detonate a full-scale Middle East war.

The terrorists could have come from the Kingdom of Jordan, whose territories at the time included the West Bank. They also could have come from Egypt and its Gaza Strip territories. Both had previously been sources for recurrent infiltration.

Both Jordan and Egypt insisted that the attackers had definitely *not* come from their territories. Each blamed the other. Their spokesmen also coyly suggested that perhaps some Arab Bedouin from within Israel had perpetrated the crime, as a protest against the creation of the Jewish state.

In Israel, the entire nation was enraged. The cabinet met in emergency session. The government was under enormous pressure to identify the perpetrators and to exact revenge. But the leaders were at a loss. Did the murderers come from the east (Jordan) or from the west (Egypt)? Or perhaps from some other direction altogether? Unless an answer were found, the government could find itself in an unprecedented crisis of confidence, this in a country not yet six years old.

The army and police carefully scoured the scene of the massacre. They brought in dogs and trackers. The hard ground showed no footprints or tracks. The police and army picked through the wreckage, but could identify no leads.

The commanding officer made his decision. There was only one man who could track the murderers and identify their place of origin and hiding. Only one man who could settle the mystery: which country had been the base from whose territory the murderers had infiltrated? Only one person who could answer the question that was already boiling over into one of the worst international political crises of the era.

He called in the Scout.

*   *   *   *

There is a hot desert wind from the east blowing outside. In the Bible, winds from the east always are omens of evil. It is a *hamsin*, a day of unusual heat, the sort that occurs in the transitional periods between spring and summer or between summer and fall. What Californians call Santa Anas. The word *hamsin* is Arabic for 50, although it has been thoroughly integrated into modern Hebrew. The basis for the term is the presumption that there are 50 such days each year, when the wind brings in the parched dry heat and dust from the Jordanian, Syrian and Saudi deserts.

I am sitting by a computer terminal with my research assistant, grinding numbers and running statistical regressions. We call it the KGB method of statistical analysis: if you torture the data enough, they always confess. My desktop computer automatically switches open an internet online bluegrass radio station when it is booted, and people from neighboring offices invariably walk by the door complaining and asking how I can listen to such noise.

The secretary comes by with a list of reminders. Three seminar students are waiting for their grades or else they cannot graduate. The exam office needs the draft of your final examination this week. Oh and your wife called. She said to remind you that your life is not worth spit if you forget you are taking her out this evening for your anniversary. She also says the clinic called, so on the way home you should pick up the paperwork from your physical.

The *hamsin* is accompanied by low barometric pressure that

always gives me headaches. At 5:00 in the afternoon of this disgustingly hot day I am a healthy forty-nine year old father of three. We have been married for fifteen years to the exact day. My wife's family long ago made their peace with her marrying an American, relieved to discover there are some Americans who do not have green hair and wear feathers.

I have lived in Israel for most of the past 20 years. My wife and I are both academic types, teaching and writing research papers that almost no one will read. Writing things that are sure cures for insomnia.

This picture of tranquility at 5:00 o'clock in the afternoon however is a delusion. At 5:30 in the afternoon I discover I have cancer.

*　　*　　*　　*

In an article on Bedouin scouts, General David Maimon of the Israel Defense Forces describes an event that took place in the Al-Hali quarter of the Saudi Arabian desert.[1] The Bedouin who live there are of short stature, but are rugged and possess legendary scouting skills. An old man from the tribe is said to have buried a coin in the sand dunes. Several days later a different tracker from his tribe, who had not been with the old man when he buried the coin, was able to locate it and retrieve it on his own. General Maimon stated that when he first heard the story he was incredulous. Then, after studying the work of Bedouin scouts, he had become convinced that it was not far-fetched.

While studying the Bedouin tribesmen in the Great Crater area of the Negev desert, the same General Maimon came across a nine-year old Bedouin shepherd boy. The boy was the son of a famous Negev scout, and had been entrusted by his family with caring for and guarding thirty-five camels. He had been living in the desert by himself with the camels for a year. Once a week other tribesmen would bring him supplies and then leave him on his own again. He had to see to his own needs as well as to those of the animals.

---

1   Appears in Yaakov Aini and Ezra Orion, *The Bedouins*, Institute for Desert Research, Ben-Gurion University, Beer Sheba, 1988 (Hebrew).

Maimon asked the boy if he knew how to count to ten, and he could not. The General asked how he could then keep track of the animals. The boy explained that he knew each camel's face the way you would know a person's. Indeed, each camel's face was known by all of the neighboring tribesmen, so should it wander off and get lost, it would be returned to its owners.

Maimon also reports on a visit with a group of Bedouin scouts sitting around a campfire in which a rabbit was being roasted. They had no weapons or traps with them. So how did you catch the rabbit, he asked. They explained that a ten year-old boy in the tribe had captured the rabbit after tracking it to its lair. He waited by the entrance of the lair all day without moving and then, when the rabbit returned home, he simply caught it with his hand.

* * * *

It is late in the evening. I have not yet attempted to sit up straight since the surgery this morning and just want to sleep. Sleep.

There is some hullabaloo as a new patient is wheeled into the ward room, placed next to me. In the haze I sense it is an old man. People are with him, perhaps his family, speaking in a frightened Arabic. He is groaning and in pain.

The staff is doing something. Sounds of an oxygen mask. Nurses buzzing about. Discussion of injections. I drift off.

* * * *

Three sons of a Bedouin sheikh were on a journey.[2] When they come to a pasture of grass, one son said that the camel who has been eating here is blind in one eye. The second son said the camel is also cross-eyed. The third said the camel has had its tail cut off. Soon thereafter they see a man on a mare, out searching. They ask if he seeks a camel who is blind in one eye, cross-eyed, and whose tail has been cut off. The man swears to Allah that this is indeed his camel and asks them where the animal is. We have not seen it at all, they answer.

They continued together on their way until they come to the tent

---

2 Story told in *"Evening Discourses"* by Yehuda Ratzbi.

of a great Bedouin chief. The man on the mare submitted a complaint
to the sheikh that the three youths had found his camel but were pre-
tending they had not seen it, in spite of their exact knowledge of it.
When questioned, the youths explained that they knew it was blind
in one eye from the way it ate the grass. They knew it was cross-eyed
from its hoof prints in the dust. They knew it had no tail from the
dung piles it had left. The man on the mare was ordered to apologize
and host the three youths at a feast in their honor.[3]

*   *   *   *

There are two related and parallel stories in the Bible about scouting
out the land. The first involves the sending out of a team of scouts by
Moses, as the Israelites approach the Promised Land. Moses however
makes a mess of things. He is a politician, always on the lookout for
how the cantankerous tribesmen will react, constantly dealing with
their bickering. He is also a diplomat. He forms a scouting expedition whose structure reflects his desire to maintain political balance,
with a representative from each tribe. The scouts are chosen no doubt
based on political clout, not professional talent. It is the world's first
affirmative action program.

The result is a debacle. The scouts come back with disinforma-
tion, recounting Paul Bunyon tales of ferocious giants in the Promised
Land. They bring to mind the joke about how a camel is really a horse
planned by a committee. They discourage the Israelites, who are ready
to head back to slavery in Egypt in their dismay.

The scouting expedition sent out by Moses is a demonstration of
how to do things with maximum confusion and minimal effective-
ness. But shortly thereafter, a different demonstration of how to do
things correctly is described.

Moses' disciple, Joshua the son of Nun, takes over command
after the death of the Teacher. Where Moses is a politician and a
diplomat, Joshua is an efficient military professional. No committees

---

3 A slightly different version of this story appears in Yaakov Habakuk, "Sand, Shadow and
   Time," *Mishkafayim*, 31, December 1995, pp. 70–71. In this version, the youths also identify the fact that the camel is carrying dates.

for him. No worrying about dainty feelings of representativeness. He sends off two professional scouts, men who do not worry about politics and niceties. They quickly return with a professional evaluation. No Paul Bunyons out there. The Canaanites are already shivering in their thongs at the approach of Israel. Piece of cake.

*   *   *   *

It is two or three in the morning and the ward is quiet, except for some dinging and buzzing of monitors of some sort. The old Arab next to me is struggling for air. He is weakly calling Nurse Nurse. He is coughing and wheezing. We are in intensive care, in the room directly opposite the nurse station, placed so that we are in direct eye contact with the staff at all times, in case we need something urgently. But the nurses are not responding. They are down the corridor, seeing to something or perhaps chatting with friends.

I hit the call button pinned to the rail. No response.

His breathing is getting more desperate. I try to pull myself to a sitting position. There are no chains or poles near the bed I can grasp, with which to use my arms to raise myself, and without them it is hopeless. My abdomen was sliced apart a few hours ago and the muscles refuse to obey, the pain too intense.

Near my bed is a hospital bedpan, a patient potty, left nearby earlier in the evening by the nurses, on the theory that discretion is the better part of valor. I manage to 3grasp it and take aim at the doorway. I must be the only American in Israel who never plays baseball. But I toss it into the empty corridor, where it lands in a cacophony in the otherwise near-silence, no doubt waking the dozens of other patients in the ward.

The startled nurses race down the corridor to see what is behind the racket. He can't breath I mutter, already drifting back into purple morphine haze. Help him.

11. The Nobility

ROSH PINA, or The Cornerstone, was one of the very first Jewish immigrant villages built in Palestine near the end of the nineteenth century. Its name comes from the verse in Psalms, "The stone that was despised by the masons became the cornerstone (of the Temple of God)." It was a small farming village, isolated in the Upper Galilee, carving out an impoverished existence, propped up by subsidies from the Rothschild family in Europe. Its residents were refugees from Czarist Russia and Poland, almost all of them small tradesmen and craftsmen, products of urban lives in Europe who were now forcing their bodies and their souls to adapt to the tribulations of farming under the harsh conditions of the backward Ottoman Empire.

Their neighbors were a tribe of Bedouin, that had migrated into Palestine from Syria two hundred years earlier. Under the Turks, these Bedouin continued to practice their age-old traditions of sheep rustling and brigandage against caravans.

One day the head of the al-Heib Bedouin tribe, unrelated to the Saadiya, had been summoned to Acre to face the cruel Turkish *Pasha*, Ahmed Jazar, who demanded that the Bedouin stop annoying the passing Turkish trade caravans. The sheikh replied that the Bedouin had been practicing this trade since time immemorial and were not about to stop now. They were simply "wetting their beaks," as it might called in a Hollywood gangster movie. The *Pasha* had him executed, boiled his body, and dropped it in front of the rest of the Bedouin entourage.

The *Pasha* then demanded from the other Bedouin to swear to Allah that they would desist from the piracy. They too refused. Fearing the consequences of further confrontation, the *Pasha* gave in. He also granted them lands on which to build their village.

*   *   *   *

The Saadiya are a tribe of Bedouin whose origins are in the *Hijaz* region of what is today Saudi Arabia. They are related to the clan of the Prophet himself, who was of the Hashim within the Quraysh (shark) tribe. Among the descendents of the Hashemites are the royal families in Jordan and in Morocco today. When a visitor from Morocco once met the Scout's family, one of the Saadiya asked if the visitor had enough influence with the King of Morocco to arrange a good position for him there. The visitor broke into laughter. "*You* are asking *me* to obtain favors in Morocco? But you are Saadiya. *You* are nobles. It is I who should be asking *you* to arrange for favors for myself from the King of Morocco!"

The *Hijaz* is the area that contains the holy cities of Mecca and Medina, the area in which the Prophet Mohammed lived and preached, the places to which Moslems make pilgrimage or *haj*. The boy Mohammed was an orphan, his father having died before he was born. His mother arranged for a Bedouin wet nurse to care for the child, as was custom at the time, and to raise him in the purity of the desert. Her name was Halima al-Saadiya, and she was from the Banu Sa'd tribe.

The Saadiya Bedouins trace their origin back to her and to the Banu Sa'd. It is said that she was among the first to recognize the holiness of Mohammed and his mission, long before the Koran was revealed to him by Allah through the angel Gabriel. She saw that he possessed a *baraka*, a mysterious blessing and force from Allah.

*   *   *   *

When the Arab armies swept across North Africa to the Atlantic, there were Saadiya among them. When the scout led the first Moslem army across the straits of Gibraltar and into Spain, these Saadiya were settled in the Maghreb, the western district of the Moslem world that encompasses Morocco, Tunisia and Algeria. Another part of the family moved to the east and settled in Jeba, a town in Syria. Jeba became the headquarters of the clan in the Levant. It was a walled town with a single gate, through which no one but a member of the Saadiya might be admitted.

*   *   *   *

As a youth, the future Prophet Mohammed was sent off to live with Bedouin near Mecca. It was considered the preferred form of education, which would toughen up the boy. He was adept at handling camels, and later made a living in this profession.

There is an Islamic legend that Mohammed underwent surgery by angels while living in the desert with the Bedouins. While playing with his foster brother, three angels in white robes suddenly appeared and laid him on his back. One of them was Jibril or Gabriel, and a second was Mikail or Michael. They took out the boy's heart and squeezed from it a black drop of liquid, the drop of sin, then washed the heart with special water they had brought in a bottle from Paradise. This purified the heart, which was returned to the boy's chest with no scar at all.[4]

*   *   *   *

In the 18th century, there lived in Syria a young man from the Saadiya named Saad a-Din. He rose to become one of the most powerful sheikhs of his people. He was both clan head and religious leader. He possessed ancient holy books, which described the cures for any illness, books that had been handed down from father to son. He treated ailments with combinations of folk remedies and religious incantations.

Saad a-Din had an additional vocation: he was an exorcist of *djinn*, of evil demon genies. Using the ancient books and simple tools, such as a metal pole, it was said that he could drive the *djinn* from the body of one possessed, forcing it out from the little toe of its host

---

4   Taken from Knappert, Jan, *Islamic Legends*, Leiden: E.J. Brill, 1985.

victim. His expertise in exorcism was taught to other family members. A cousin of the Scout still practices exorcism in the Galilee today.

*   *   *   *

It is late at night. In a few hours I will undergo the surgery.

The night before he was to confront Esau on his return from Syria, Jacob had one of the strangest experiences in the Bible. He is not sure whether Esau, his twin brother, is still determined to murder him for having taken away the family birthright and blessing. Jacob has been hiding from his brother for two decades in the far north, where he married and raised a large family. In the morning he will face the moment of truth on the plains. He does not know whether he will come out of it alive.

In the evening before the confrontation with fate, Jacob sends off his family and servants. The Bible says, "And Jacob was left alone." Entirely, utterly alone. It is one of the simplest, yet most haunting, sentences in the Bible. He must face his moment of destiny with absolutely no one to assist him. With no one he can beseech, at least no *person*.

During the night he is confronted by a strange one, a messenger or an angel. Some say it was God Himself. They wrestle with one another the entire night, until dawn breaks. Jacob wins, but emerges injured, limping. For thousands of years his descendents will wrestle with God and often emerge maimed.

*   *   *   *

In times of imminent danger and threats of destruction, Jews congregate in the synagogue and say a special prayer, pleading with God for salvation. The Jews of the town of Rosh Pina gathered in their synagogue in tears and panic. The Angel of Death was approaching them in the dust.

The body of a Bedouin youth had been found in one of their fields. The Bedouin were renowned for their ferocious vendettas and blood vengeance, and the tribe in the nearby village had long surpassed all the others in its bouts of vindictive rage. The discovery of the youth, brutally murdered, in the fields of the Jews would endanger their very existence in Rosh Pina and threaten them with annihilation. They were

refugees from Eastern Europe, and feared the pogrom had at last caught
up with them, tracked them down here in the Galilee. The Jews had
only a tiny handful of arms, and a pathetic militia of guardsmen, no
match for the ferocious warriors of the Bedouin tribe.

A party of Bedouin was approaching Rosh Pina, led by the Sheikh
Muhammed al-Ali. Al-Ali never went anywhere without a full contingent of tribesmen armed to the teeth. Until now, his relations with the
Jews had always been cordial. When he rode through the main street
of Rosh Pina, the Jews stood and greeted him with respect and offered
him water from their well. But al-Ali was also famous throughout the
Galilee for his violent passions and obsession with blood vengeance.

The Jews gathered to pray in the synagogue of Rosh Pina, asking
for deliverance. Al-Ali entered the town to learn that all the menfolk
were huddled in the synagogue. He rode there directly, at the head
of his band of fighters. At the synagogue gate, he dismounted and
handed his rifle to one of his subordinates. He entered the synagogue
as the Jews prepared to recite the last prayer before death, Hear O
Israel, the Lord Our God, the Lord is One. Seeing the fear in their
eyes, the Sheikh announced, "My brothers, the farmers of Rosh Pina.
Have no fear. We know you did not kill the youth."

The congregation rushed to embrace the Sheikh. Some Arab
peasants in a nearby village had murdered the Bedouin youth when
he had tried to steal some grain from their threshing area. Fearing the
wrath of the Bedouin, they had moved the body to the field of Rosh
Pina, hoping to deflect the violence onto the Jews. The Sheikh was on
his way now to extract vengeance from the dogs.[5]

*   *   *   *

"The longevity of life is from Allah,
the quality of life is from one's neighbors."

— Arab folk saying.

*   *   *   *

---

5   Source for story: Saul Dagan and Avner Kozviner, "Palheib: Bedouins in the Palmach in
    1948," The Yigal Alon Center for the History of the Hagana Force, Yad Tabenkin, 1993
    (Hebrew).

There is a Jewish legend (in *Breishit Raba*) that when the Patriarch Abraham was born, the evil king of his home city in Iraq saw omens that Abraham would grow up to end paganism on earth and sought to kill him, to prevent this from happening. But Abraham's family hid the child for three years in a cave. At the age of three, the child emerged from the cave. He looked up at the sun and thought, "This must be God". But the sun set. He then looked up at the moon and thought, This must be God, but the moon set. He concluded that there must be a single God above and behind both, who created the two.

Rabbi Shimon Bar Yochai, one of the greatest of sages in the Talmud, is traditionally credited with having written the masterpiece of Jewish mysticism, the *Zohar*. He also asks how it could be that in a world where everyone was a pagan, Abraham nevertheless discovered monotheism. Bar Yochai explains that God granted wisdom to Abraham through his kidneys. God filled them with wisdom as if they were jugs of water.

*   *   *   *

Saad a-Din had several sons. One of them was named Abdul-Rahman. Leaving behind most of his family in Syria, he traveled south into Palestine with his brother Salim. The brother settled with his family in the area of Zippori (or Sepphoris), while Abdul-Rahman moved further west, to the Raaba area in the lower Galilee. There were almost no settlements in this area back then, just green fields and pasture. There he met and fell in love with a local Bedouin girl. They married, had four children, and began their own Bedouin dynasty in that part of the country. They lived in tents, herded animals, did some farming.

Abdul-Rahman raised four sons and a daughter. His son Hassan married twice, raising eleven children in all. He and others from his family worked part of the time as guardsmen for the lands of the German Templar colonies of the Galilee. He would sleep days and patrol the lands at night from horseback, armed with a hunting rifle and bandolier.

One night, at around 2:00 AM, Hassan was out patrolling the

lands of the Germans, fields in which their herds grazed. He spotted a group of thieves trying to make off with one of the cows belonging to the Templar colony. He aimed his hunting rifle and killed one of the thieves with a single shot. The others fled.

The dead thief turned out to be a Bedouin youth from a rival clan, the Masawiya. Once the news had spread, the entire Masawiya began to march in the direction of the Saadiya encampment to extract revenge, to make them pay in blood for the death of the youth. But the further on they marched, the more time they had to consider the risks of confronting the powerful Saadiya.

What happened next is not altogether clear. But shortly thereafter the entire Masawiya returned to their own encampment without having fired off a single shot. The vengeance party swore that when they had approached the tents of the Saadiya, suddenly a colossal figure descended from Heaven. It was an enormous sheikh, a giant, whose head – crowned by a white *Lafa* – was in the clouds. It was from Allah. He would not countenance a revenge attack. They had no choice but to retreat.

A few days later, the Masawiya contacted the Saadiya and asked to conduct with them a *sulkh*, a ceremony of reconciliation.

*   *   *   *

He was the epitome of wisdom, understanding and kindness. In an era of greatness, Rabbi Saadiya of Sura stood above all the rest. He was the Gaon of Babylon, the greatest Jewish scholar of the ninth century. Born in Egypt, he translated the Bible into Arabic and wrote philosophical treatises in Hebrew and Arabic. His book of prayers still forms the basis for Jewish prayer throughout the world.

Once, Rabbi Saadiya traveled to a distant town on a communal matter. He arrived late at night, made his way to the local Jewish inn and requested lodging. The innkeeper, not recognizing his guest, tossed a key at him and pointed to a room at the end of the corridor.

The next morning, as the innkeeper made his way through the local bazaar, he noticed that all the shops of the Jewish merchants were closed. He didn't understand. He knew there was no holiday that day. Arriving at the synagogue, he found the entire community gathered to hear the famed Gaon deliver a lecture. When the innkeeper saw that the distinguished sage was none other than his guest of the previous night, he became disconsolate. "How could I have treated him so poorly," he berated himself over and over.

At the end of the lecture, the innkeeper raced to the podium from which Rabbi Saadiya had been speaking, threw himself to the floor at his feet, and began to wail, begging for forgiveness. "If I had only known who you were", he sobbed, "I would have served you so much better."

Some years later, a disciple of Rabbi Saadiya discovered him alone in his room weeping, lamenting and pounding his chest with his fists. The disciple didn't reveal his presence, but looked on in wonderment and confusion. He finally summoned the courage to ask Rabbi Saadiya for an explanation of his unusual behavior. "I am seeking repentance," admitted the Rabbi.

"But surely," protested the disciple, "the Gaon is not in need of such! The Gaon is engaged without interruption the entire day and night in study of the Holy Books. How could it be that such repentance is needed?" Rabbi Saadiya sighed and smiled. He told the student the story of the innkeeper that had occurred years earlier.

"You see, yesterday I was reminded of that old story and I suddenly understood. I realized that I barely know God. If I had only known yesterday what I know now, how magnificent is the Master of the World, how great is His kindness, and how much we are required to praise Him and express our gratitude, I would surely have served Him so much better."

Rabbi Saadiya died at a young age. In *his* first jubilee year.

*　*　*　*

One day Sheikh Muhammed was walking through the town of Safed in the Galilee when he bumped into his friend, the Jew Joseph Friedman. While chatting on the street, several Arabs approached the Sheikh. They told him about how the Moslems in Safed were building a mosque but had run out of funds, and asked if he would make a contribution to allow the work to be resumed. Naturally they did not ask Friedman for a contribution. But hearing of the problem,

Friedman himself volunteered to make his own contribution to assist in the construction.

The story of the contribution by the Jew Friedman to the construction fund for the mosque spread and eventually reached the ears of the Sultan himself, Abdul Hamid II, in Istanbul. He sent Friedman a royal sword and shield as symbols of respect, and as signs that Friedman enjoyed royal favor.

iii. The Germans

GERMAN PIETISM arose as an evangelical reform movement within Protestantism in the seventeenth century. It was particularly strong in the southern German state of Wurttemberg. Among the early Pietists a popular prophesy arose holding that Christ Himself would return to earth in the year 1837, a belief that quickly put them at odds with other Protestants. Some of the Pietists migrated east, to the Caucasus mountains, where they awaited Judgement Day. Others set up their own separate communities within Germany, segregated from the outside world.[6]

Still others migrated to the New World. In particular, a large group built a town outside of colonial Philadelphia in the 18th century, called Germantown. It was there that George Washington fought a bloody battle against the British during the American War of Independence, a few days after the Battle of the Clouds.

The Battle of Germantown went badly for the Americans because of poor scouting. Washington attempted to coordinate an attack by four separate units of troops. The British were camped at Cliveden Manor, on whose grounds I collected autumn leaves with my friends as a child. The logistics were too much for the Americans, and the battle was lost.

I was born in that Germantown, long since incorporated into Philadelphia. My father was a refugee from Germany, who fled

---

6 The historic details of the Templar movement are based on Alex Carmel, *German Settlement in the Land of Israel at the End of the Ottoman Era*, Institute for the Study of Christian Activity in Palestine in the 19th Century, University of Haifa, 1990 (Hebrew).

the Nazis and arrived in New York Harbor in early 1938 with a few
dollars in his pocket, speaking almost no English. His parents, my
grandparents, stayed behind in Germany and were murdered by the
Nazis. When the United States entered the War, he became a GI and
served in Patton's regiments, blasting their way across France and into
the Rheinland.

*   *   *   *

In one of the Pietist communities in Wurttemberg, Christoph Hoffman was born in 1815. By the late 1840s he had gained fame as a prom-
inent and controversial preacher, author and parliamentary deputy. In
his writings he seemed obsessed with assorted manifestations of the
fulfillment of biblical prophesies in the contemporary world. It was
exactly 400 years since Constantinople had been conquered by the
Ottomans, and the Saracens were lately being pushed backwards and
out of Europe in a series of wars with the Russians. It was expected
that the Holy Land itself, the birthplace of Christ, would soon be
liberated from Saracen control.

When the Crimean War broke out, in which Russia and Turkey
(among others) went to war, many believed the hour of destiny had
arrived. And who better to take the place of the defeated Sultan and
his Janissaries in the Holy Land than the elected People of God, the
German Pietists themselves!

In the year 1852, Hoffman and some associates held their first
conference in Berlin, where Hoffman's brother served as spiritual
advisor to the Prussian Kaiser. They issued a call to Pietists to migrate
to the Holy Land in fulfillment of the Biblical prophesies and prepare
themselves for Christ's imminent arrival. Their theology aroused the
anger of the mainstream Protestant orders, even including the major-
ity of Pietists, who insisted that the prophesies regarding the imminent gathering of the dispersed to Palestine were referring to the Jews
and not to Christians. The establishment churches shunned the new
movement and its leaders. Nevertheless the order in Germany grew
to 10,000 souls by 1854.

The movement called itself the Order of Templars, named after
the Medieval Order of Knights who had fought the Saracens during

the Crusades. The Crusader Templars had been followers of Saint Bernard, themselves named after the Temple of Jerusalem built by King Solomon, near the site of which they established their headquarters after butchering their way into Jerusalem in the year 1099.

The Pietist Templars of the 19th century crisscrossed Germany, drumming up support for their new crusade to establish evangelical colonies in the Holy Land. Hoffman, now called the Templar Bishop, took to the road in 1858 with two other leaders to explore the Holy Land, in a mission seen by them as very much like that of the scouts sent out by Moses.

They arrived in the port of Jaffa, the very place from which the Prophet Jonah had sailed, shortly after a massacre of German and American colonists in the area by Arabs. One of the victims of that attack was named Steinbeck, perhaps a distant relation of the great author of Salinas. Like the scouts sent out by Moses, they returned with a pessimistic, discouraging picture. The situation in Palestine was not ripe for colonization by the People of God. Instead, they would have to restrict themselves to intensified missionary activity in the Holy Land.

Four new agents were then sent to Palestine. Of these, one became a Moslem, one joined a missionary order hostile to the Templars, one died of malaria, and one simply disappeared.

The year 1866 began as a dismal year for the Templars. Wurttemberg was allied with the France of Napoleon III against Prussia, and the Templars regarded the French King as the Antichrist himself. Many of the younger members of the Order escaped to America or elsewhere to dodge the Wurttemberg military conscription. Almost as discouraging, the Templars had just been upstaged by a group of 156 American Christian colonists who had moved to Palestine as the avant-garde of the Redemption. (Most of these gave up in defeat within a few months of arrival in the face of the primitive living conditions and returned to America.)

Meanwhile Henry Dunant, the founder of the Red Cross, was stealing the thunder of the Templars by urging Europeans to colonize the East, and even the Jews were making efforts to organize migration to Palestine. Finally, the French banker on whom the Templars

were counting for finance decided his money was better invested in
Algeria.

It was only in 1868 when the first Templar colonists actually
trickled into Palestine, and even these managed quickly to get into
conflict with one another. Bishop Hoffman moved his family to Jaffa,
while others remained in Haifa. With its 4,000 people, Haifa was an
attractive alternative because of its proximity to the Mediterranean,
although its seafront was little more than a small fishing port. Haifa
offered the means of rapid escape, if such proved necessary.

The more important port was in Acre, nearby up the coast. Napoleon had used Haifa only as a way station, hospital and supply depot
on his failed march from Alexandria in Egypt to Acre in 1799. He had
been stopped cold at the outskirts of Acre by the Moslems in a sort
of Battle of Germantown, whence he escaped to Europe to emerge as
the Greatest of Emperors. The battleground in Acre is still referred to
as Napoleon's Hill.

*   *   *   *

A block or two away from Napoleon's Hill is a hotel next to the sea.
Fifteen years ago I was married there. By Israeli standards it was a very
small affair, with not many more than 300 guests. Standing under the
hupa, the canopy and symbolic house formed by a prayer shawl under
which the bride and groom take their vows, I pulled out a guitar and
sang to the bride before the guests. A song of biblical metaphors, set
to the tune of an old Bukharan folksong. The pomegranate tree grants
its aroma, from the Dead Sea to Jericho, the treasures of Ophir and
the balm of Gilead, the chariots of Egypt, all have I captured for you,
my lass. A thousand melodies will serve as your shield, from the Nile
to the Jordan. For you the trumpeting, for you the wreaths, for you
all the medallions of the heroes, to you and for you the warrior yearns,
come my bride for evening falls.

*   *   *   *

Hassan's second child was named Suleiman, the Arabic name for
Solomon, the wisest of men, who plays an even larger role in the
Koran than he does in the Bible. Suleiman spent his days caring for

his herds and fields. Like his father, he also worked for the Templars, helping them to guard their lands. He lived in a shack near the fields he guarded. Four sons had been born when his first wife died.

One day, an official for the Jewish National Fund named Jacob Salomon approached Suleiman. He was buying up lands in the vicinity, lands on which the Jewish authorities hoped to set up settlements for Jewish immigrants and refugees arriving in Palestine. Salomon was a lawyer and rancher based on Mount Carmel and a leader in the Zionist organizations. He had heard that Suleiman was the most powerful Bedouin sheikh in the region, and that his clan – the Saadiya – were the most feared.

The two Solomons (that is, Salomon and Suleiman) met and became friends. Suleiman agreed to work for Salomon as a guardsman for lands being purchased. He and his clan would keep the local peasants from raiding, stealing from cultivated fields, or squatting on the Jewish lands.

*   *   *   *

The eldest son of Suleiman was named Salim, born in 1924. The *Zohar*, the Jewish book of mysticism and *kabbala*, attributes great importance to the selection of a child's name by parents. When the parents select a name, it is not only for their child, for they are also naming the child's soul. In so doing, they are dictating personality traits and characteristics that will develop later on.

"Salim" means peaceful. It comes from the same Arabic linguistic root as *Salaam* and Suleiman, and the word Islam. It is essentially the same as the Hebrew linguistic root for *Shalom* and its cognates, including the name Solomon, the name Shiloh, and the name of the city of peace, *Yeru-shalem* or Jerusalem.

*   *   *   *

When Salim was weaned, a celebration was organized. A basket of sweets was brought in for the child. But when the backs of the family were turned, a she-goat discovered the sweets and gorged herself. She paid the price for the theft. She died that night from overeating.

Salim lived with his father and brothers in their hut. There was no running water in those days, only a well from which the families in the vicinity carried water home in clay jugs. He wore a traditional Bedouin robe, a *Galabiya*, and often went barefoot. He did not own his first pair of trousers until adulthood. All of his clothes were hand sewn at home by the womenfolk of the clan.

Salim would bake pita for his younger brothers on a *saj*, an iron plate on which the dough was spread. Old women from among the Bedouin acted as midwives and as healers for the children, using folk remedies, smoke, fire, olive oil, and herbs to cure ailments. Once, when the boy was taken seriously ill, the family threw a mattress onto the back of the horse wagon and took him into Haifa for medical care.

His formal schooling lasted for only a short period. It consisted of lessons by an old itinerate Bedouin teacher with poor eyesight, known as Blind Jamil. Salim and a few other youths from the region would walk by foot to the tent of the old man. They would catch grasshoppers along the way and occasionally birds' eggs and bring them to the teacher, who would fry them for his lunch. The children learned arithmetic and how to read and write in Arabic.

*   *   *   *

When I moved to Haifa from the Midwest, I lived in a neighborhood composed mainly of older German Jews. They had arrived before, during and after World War ii. German Jews are notorious in Israel for having difficulty in picking up Hebrew. Many in the neighborhood still spoke nothing but German after decades of living in the country. A joke has it that a group of German Jews walking on the beach promenade see a pal in the ocean flapping his arms and screaming in Hebrew *help* HELP; they simply respond, "Hey, if you are smart enough to learn Hebrew then you are smart enough to learn how to swim."

I nicknamed the neighborhood Germantown, and in some cases was forced to speak to the neighbors in my own broken German, sometimes better than their Hebrew. The German Jews are fastidious dressers, the only people in the country who wear ties and berets. The sidewalks here are spotless in otherwise littered Israel, and God help

the children who make noises between 2:00 and 4:00 in the afternoon, the official siesta hours.

Kestler's is the great secret of the insiders in the neighborhood.
The best bakery and coffee spot in the city. It sits in the back of an
alley off the main avenue, hidden from view. Only the locals even
know it exists. They sit and chat in German and sometimes Romanian or English. My wife and I like to take mid-week breaks there.
After the coffee I always get up and say to her in a loud voice, "Just
be careful your husband does not find out!" The denizens of the cafe
stare at us wide-eyed as we walk away giggling.

Once the elderly woman from downstairs called me to the stairwell. The one who always refused to call me by my first name, insist-
ing on calling me Herr Professor. There was a horrible smelly brown
stain all over the walls of the stairwell. She was trying to explain to
me what it was, but did not know the Hebrew words. Let me guess,
I say in German, it is bat droppings, recalling the German word for
bat from the operetta *Die Fledermaus*. She is astonished I know the
word.

Later, after I am married, she insists on calling my wife Frau Professor. She lightens up only after my daughter is born. During Israel's
War of Independence, she and her husband hid and operated a small
storage "slick" of weapons for the Hagana.

*   *   *   *

The Templars in Haifa slowly erected a neighborhood of stone houses
that is still referred to as the German Colony. It contained keepers
of vineyards, farmers, architects, a construction engineer, flour mill
workers, and a special group of tour guides for pilgrims.

The Templars improved the roads nearby and introduced horse
and donkey-drawn wagon transportation, which had been previously
unknown in Haifa. There had simply been no roads on which the
wagons could pass. Indeed the greatest master of artillery, Napoleon
himself, had lost the battle of Acre because he had to leave all his
heavier artillery pieces behind in Egypt for lack of roads. The Templars began the first carriage service between Haifa and Acre, and then
between Haifa and Nazareth. Arabs from the Nazareth area shared in

the road expenses. The Templars' houses and their *Gemeindehaus*, or meeting house, were built by hired Arab construction workers. Above the entrance to the meeting house was engraved the inscription in German, "If I should forget Jerusalem let my right hand forget its cunning," from the 137th Psalm. It is the same pledge I made under the *hupa* at the Acre beach hotel, the words that complete any Jewish wedding ceremony.

*   *   *   *

The Templars settled in and expanded. New Templar colonies were built in Jaffa and Jerusalem. The Haifa Templars built summer residences to escape the heat at the crest of Mount Carmel, forming the basis of what would later be my own "Germantown" neighborhood. The neighborhood synagogue today is in one of the old Templar buildings.

They were extremely enthusiastic hosts for the German Kaiser Wilhelm II, who visited Palestine at the end of the nineteenth century. It was the first time a German King had stepped on the soil of the Holy Land since the Crusader Knight Frederick II, 670 years earlier. In his honor the Templars established a new farming colony, Wilhelma.

But they were finding themselves increasingly divided theologically, and parts of their community were being swept up by the new German nationalism triggered by the unification of Bismarck. Nevertheless their colonies continued to expand. In 1906 and 1907 the Haifa Templars established two new agricultural colonies near the pass into the Jezreel Valley, not far from where Elijah had defied King Ahab and where Deborah led the Israelites to victory.

The lands for the new colonies were purchased from an Arab aristocrat, an *effendi* living in Lebanon named Tuani, for 130,000 francs. The colonies were named Galilean Bethlehem and Waldheim. They were built close to the archeological remains of the Roman town of Beit Shearim, which was once the home of the great Judah the Prince, one of the greatest rabbis of all ages, the redactor of the *Mishnah*.

Bethlehem means "house of bread," and the full name – Galilean Bethlehem – was to distinguish it from the town with the similar name in which Jesus was born. In biblical times it had been known as the Bethlehem of Tyre because it was under the domination of the Lebanese Phoenicians. It is mentioned in the Book of Joshua.

The name of the second new colony, Waldheim, is German for the "forests of home." It was established by "dissident" Templars who had broken with the main movement and were seeking reconciliation with mainstream Pietism. The lands around the new colonies were empty except for encampments of Bedouin.

The new Galilee colonies were slow to develop. The Ottoman authorities were suspicious of any further expansion by the Templars, as was the Kaiser's government in Berlin. The colonists suffered from malaria and their crops were often stolen. After a thief was shot by a Templar sentry, Arabs murdered Fritz Unger, one of the leaders in the colony, in revenge.

The Templars also faced militant opposition from the Carmelites, a Catholic – mostly French – order of monks, whose headquarters and monasteries were nearby on Mount Carmel. The last thing the monks wanted was a swarm of heretic Protestant mystics on their turf.

The political position of the colonists was precarious. The Templars were dependent on the Ottomans for protection. The German government and the Turks were on friendly terms with one another and were collaborating in the construction of the first rail lines from Istanbul to Mecca and Baghdad, with a spur that would pass through Haifa. The Templars were hostile to the Jewish immigrants flowing into the country, largely due to theological disapproval of the aims of Zionism, partly also due to fears of economic competition and suspicions that the Zionists were getting too cozy with the British. The Jews built competing vineyards and wineries on the southern flanks of Mount Carmel.

Meanwhile the Templar relationship with other Christians in the Holy Land was becoming explosive. In 1900, a group of Arab Catholics attacked an Ottoman army unit protecting the Haifa port wharf near the German Colony, the same pier that had been built to allow the Kaiser to land in Haifa in regal glory. The Templars claimed that the Arabs had been incited by the French Carmelite Catholics. They offered the Turkish troops refuge. In response, the Arabs attacked the entire German colony. The violence broke out because the Arab Catholics saw the German Protestants as allies of the Turkish infidels.

When World War I broke out, the Templar colonists supported the Germans and their Turkish allies. The Templar menfolk were conscripted for the war effort. A French warship appeared in Haifa bay and shelled the Templar colony. The Turks meanwhile avenged themselves on the French Carmelite monks, ordering them to vacate Mount Carmel, and invited German and Austrian monks to take their places. The graves of the troops of Napoleon, buried on the grounds of the monastery, were sacked by thieves. Meanwhile, the British army of General Allenby systematically punched its way through Palestine, expelling the Turks from the Holy Land, leaving the Templars under the military control of their country's enemy.

*   *   *   *

It must be close to midnight. About twelve hours have drifted past since the surgery. I am one kidney lighter than I was upon awakening this morning. I have been passing in and out of consciousness since returning to the ward from the surgery, high on morphine. I keep asking the nurses if this is Woodstock.

Only ten days have passed since the discovery of the tumor. It was a mass the size of a tennis ball. The diagnosis seemed so harmless at first: RCC. An acronym that sounds like the name of some sort of cola. Hey, get yer ice-cold RCC Cola, folks! Actually, RCC is renal cell carcinoma.

Those ten days are now a blur, a whirlwind of rushing about to get further tests done, of attacking the bureaucratic challenges of getting slow institutions to move in the country's socialist health system. It is a system that has been on strike for weeks over wage demands. And it has also been a period of infuriating sitting about and waiting uselessly, pointlessly, impotently.

I suppose that whenever a father goes into the hospital for major surgery, family briefings are routinely conducted. The wife is drilled and run through the basics of various important matters. Where the family's money is sitting. How to transfer funds and write checks in various currencies. How appliances work. How to do this and where to find that.

Our pre-hospitalization briefings are somewhat different. My wife is an engineer and certainly more competent than me in the technicalities of how things work. She also needs little instruction in financial management. What she needs though is my secret sabbath chicken recipe.

Since we were married, my household responsibilities include the Friday afternoon cooking and preparations for the sabbath. No food is cooked or baked from sunset on Friday until darkness on Saturday night. I have my own secret recipe that has been in the family for zero generations. Leftover from my bachelor days, it is based on preparing reasonably tasty food with a minimum of effort and time investment. I have always refused to reveal the secret details. But now, alas, the time has come.

*   *   *   *

When Salim was nine, his father remarried. He wanted a woman in the house to help raise his young sons. His new bride was a woman very much his junior. Things did not work out as planned. From the start there were frictions in the house between the new mistress and the children. She would beat them and there was constant bickering. One day she beat one of the younger boys so badly Salim believed his life was in danger. As the nine-year old eldest son, he could not stand by. He protested before his father, but the father sided with his wife.

In a rage, Salim fled the house. He hiked into the forest and slept that night on the bough of a tree. He had no water or food with him. The next day he stayed all day in the forest until the senselessness of having left home without any food was becoming painfully obvious to him. He waited until evening and then tried to slip back into his father's house to take some food from the pantry.

Suddenly his father leapt out and grabbed him from behind. The boy held up his arms to deflect the imminent blows. But instead, his father embraced him and broke into tears.

It was obvious to both that some distance had to be placed between the boy and the stepmother. The solution was on hand. The family had always been on good terms with the Germans and a cousin was working there as a plowman. They would approach the Templars and ask if they would hire Salim.

*   *   *   *

Katz was a common Jewish name in Europe. It is said to have been formed from an acronym for the Hebrew words "Righteous Priest," and was invariably the name of Jews tracing their ancestry back to the *kohanim*, the priestly caste from the time of the Bible. My grandmother was born a Katz in Germany.

Fritz Katz however was a German Protestant. He was the leader of the Templar colony of Waldheim, not far from Galilean Bethlehem. Fluent in Arabic, he was referred to by most of the locals and even by the Germans themselves as the *Mukhtar*, the Arabic term for a mayor or head of a clan.

The *Mukhtar* was surprised to see his Bedouin plowman coming in that morning with a nine year-old boy behind him. Salim insisted on standing back while his cousin asked the *Mukhta*r for work for him. He preferred to be off at a distance in case the answer should be negative, lest he lose face before the other Arabs working for the Germans. He was a member of the Saadiya and did not want to appear as anything less than noble before the *fellahin*.

This is the son of Suleiman the guard, explained the cousin. The *Mukhtar's* eyes widened. He had the highest opinion of Suleiman and would be happy to employ his son. Salim could work and also join the children of Arab workers in the colony in Koran classes, taught by a teacher hired for this purpose.

Salim was too small still to work as a plowman. On the first day of the new job, he was sent to work around a threshing machine, gathering up the chaff of the wheat being dropped from the machine. The Arab peasants working in the threshing yard looked on him with suspicion. Who was this nine-year old and why was the *Mukhtar* treating him with such deference?

But the work was filthy and too difficult for the boy. The daughter of the *Mukhtar* was a 25 year-old woman named Metha. Seeing the boy's difficulty, she asked if he knew how to milk a cow. Of course, he assured her, he was a true expert and professional milker.

Salim had never milked a cow before in his life. Metha brought him into the barn and set him down alongside the largest and meanest of the milk cows, a huge black monster with a white spot on its forehead. He sat and yanked and yanked until his muscles ached. Not a drop of milk came out. Metha could hardly control her laughter. Never mind, she assured him in her fluent Arabic, you will soon be a master milker.

She then taught him to milk using the gentlest cow in the colony. Slowly his confidence grew. He had to begin work each morning at 4:00 AM, which meant that he had to get up at 2:00 AM to hike the distance from his father's home to the colony. But he had no clock or watch.

The *Mukhtar* Katz had a solution. He had an old wind-up alarm clock from Germany. He would wind it and set it each day for the boy, who would take it home, use it to wake up at night for work, and then return it the next day for the *Mukhtar* to reset.

Sunday was the Christian Sabbath, the day when the Templars rested and worshipped. Sunday was also the day when Salim would demonstrate his appreciation to the *Mukhtar* who had taken him in and given him work. He would rise as usual in the middle of the night and milk the cows. Then he would clean the yard and the paths in front of the Katz home. When Katz and his family awoke and set out for church, everything was already spotless, sparkling and orderly. Not a single disorderly leaf or pebble in the yard or path.

*   *   *   *

Salim was only ten-and-a-half when the tractor of the Templar colony broke down one day. It needed a replacement part and such parts were only available from a single distributor in Tel Aviv – the great cosmopolitan center of the country. The German *Mukhtar* asked Salim to go. He did not trust anyone else with the mission or with the money. It was 21 pounds, Palestinian pounds issued by the British Mandatory government but tied in value to British sterling. More money than the boy had ever seen in his life.

The boy had never been to Tel Aviv before, in fact had never been very far away from the vicinity of his home. And the responsibility for so large an amount of cash was crushing. He hid 20 pounds out of the total in his socks and throughout his clothing, lest he be overtaken by robbers during the mission. He kept only a single pound in his pocket, for the bus fares and related costs.

It was already afternoon when he climbed aboard the bus for the south. It was a long bus route on a broken-down vehicle from one of the Arab bus companies that operated at the time. The bus slowly worked its way south, passing through Nablus on the West Bank. Near sunset it entered Tel Aviv, the metropolis of the country, with its mind-boggling population of more than 150,000. The boy had never seen anything like it. Huge skyscrapers four stories tall. Stores and lights that illuminate the night.

But it was already evening and he would have to wait until morning to purchase the tractor part and return to the Colony. Near the Central Bus Station, he entered a restaurant to purchase his supper. There were two suspicious characters staring at him, young punks in their twenties. They invited him to come sit with them. He refused, saying he was accustomed to eating by himself. He grew increasingly uneasy from the way they were glancing at him and whispering between themselves, and the 20 pounds were ablaze in his pockets and socks.

He sneaked out the back of the restaurant and asked passersby where he could find a cheap hotel room. A rooming house was pointed out. He entered and rented a single room for the night, unwilling to share a room with any stranger.

The responsibility for the money was overwhelming. He kept himself awake all night, never dozing off, lest someone enter the room while he was unconscious. When he heard some roosters crow, he arose and dressed. He went to the address of the distributor and waited for its doors to open. Afraid to enter a restaurant, lest it also contain unsavory characters like the one the evening before, he bought his breakfast from a grocery store. He then found the bus home and presented the priceless tractor part to the *Mukhtar* that afternoon.

To this day, he makes it a part of his daily routine to spread any cash he is carrying among the various pockets in the clothes he is wearing.

* * * *

By the age of 12, he was appointed by the *Mukhtar* as foreman. He would supervise the Arab peasant workers on the farm, the *fellahin*. But they resented being bossed about by a lad still wet behind the ears. Some would soon have opportunity to vent this resentment.

When he was not busy on the farm working for the Germans, he would roam the countryside with his father, who was himself a legendary scout, as had been his grandfather and all those before them. Two of his cousins were professional scouts working for the British constabulary force in Mandatory Palestine. In 1936, his cousin Ibrahim was leading a group of British police on the tracks of some thieves near Hurshon, south of Haifa. The thieves were hiding in ambush. The scout was clearly visible, wearing a *kafiya* and leading the group. They fired. His cousin was killed.

* * * *

He was almost 20 when he fell in love with a young woman from a nearby village. But obstacles arose. His family would not approve of the match. He was from the nobility, a Saadi. She was nothing but a peasant girl. The match could not be.

Instead, the family would select an alternative bride for him. His father wanted him to marry immediately. The father was in poor health and was desperate to have a woman in the household to help care for Salim's younger brothers.

One day his father brought out two horses and took him for a ride. He pointed at a young girl. That is who you will marry, the father declared. The son had no choice but to obey.

iv. The Butcher

THE BUTCHER was born Fawzi al-Kaukji in Tripoli, Lebanon. He was sent by the Ottoman ruling authorities to study at the Military Academy in Istanbul in 1912, where he met Prince Faisal, the man who would later lead the Arab revolt against the Turks together with his friend, Lawrence of Arabia.

After graduation, al-Kaukji returned to Tripoli. During World War I he served in the Ottoman army, trying to resist the invasions of its lands by the British and French. After the War, he entered the French Foreign Legion in Lebanon, working his way up to officer status. And beginning in 1925, he joined the periodic revolts by Arabs against French colonial authority. When the Druse of Syria revolted against the French, he was among the leaders. When these revolts were suppressed, al-Kaukji fled to Saudi Arabia, and from there to Iraq.

In Baghdad in 1932, he entered the Military Academy and became an officer in the Iraqi army, which was under British imperial command and control. When riots broke out in Palestine, he set out to lead them.

From 1936 until 1939, Palestine was torn by the Great Arab Revolt, a set of pogroms and riots directed against the Jews and the British. Al-Kaukji commanded the Arab militias of the Galilee. The Templars were still living in their colonies near Haifa and these were besieged by the Arab militias and rioters, who seized the surrounding fields.

It was at this time that the Scout had his first encounter with the Butcher's men.

*　　*　　*　　*

One day Cantor, the procurement agent for the Jewish militia called the Hagana, appeared in the colony of Waldheim and asked to purchase four cows from the Germans to feed the Jewish fighters in the area. Salim and his brother Ahmed were asked by the *Mukhtar* to separate out the four designated beasts and to drive them the kilometer or so to where the Jewish forces were camped. The Germans feared trying to cross the lines of the Arab militias nearby by themselves.

The two Bedouin youths had almost reached the Jewish lines when suddenly a squad of the Butcher's militiamen materialized. Ahmed saw them first and raced to escape. While running, he was shot in the calf of his leg, but managed to get away. Salim, then 12 years old, was caught and taken to a prison operated by the militiamen. There he was beaten, interrogated, and accused of being a spy, of helping the infidel Jews. It was treason to bring food to the Hagana fighters.

Word spread quickly that the boy was imprisoned. Within hours the Saadiya were fully armed and on the march. They approached the village where the boy was being held and issued a short ultimatum to the militiamen. Moments later, the boy was freed.

Meanwhile, a member of the Saadiya who was employed as a scout for the British police suddenly appeared from out of nowhere, driving a "borrowed" British armored command car. Salim located his wounded brother and carried him out on his shoulders, loading him into the armored car. They drove to the German Templar colony in Galilean Bethlehem. There Ahmed was patched up and soon recovered.

* * * *

Abdul Majid was a shepherd boy, born in Naura in the Galilee, from the M'jareeb tribe of Bedouin. As a youth he showed extraordinary skills as a scout as well as a marksmen. He lived near the Jewish cooperative farm colony of Nahalal and was friends with the most famous person to emerge from there, the man who would later be world famous as General Moshe Dayan. He was also close friends with a Jewish commander of the Galilee guardsmen named Oded Yanai, who had adopted the Arabic name of Abu Nur, the Father of Light.

The Butcher's men were particularly suspicious of Bedouin

youths on good terms with the Jews. He issued a command for the shepherd to enlist in his militia. The youth refused. The Butcher's men then accused the young shepherd of spying for the Jews. They caught him and tossed him into a pit in the ground for three days, like Joseph in the Book of Genesis, where he was interrogated and given no food or water.

Somehow the shepherd got free. Later when the State of Israel was proclaimed, he approached the commanders of the Israel Defense Forces, as the Hagana had been renamed. He enlisted. He organized the Israeli army's first camel patrol and served as a scout. His boyhood friend Abu Nur had exchanged his Hebrew name for an Arabic one, and now the shepherd did the opposite. He adopted a Hebrew *nom de guerre*, Amos Yarkoni. He was nicknamed by the soldiers the "Father of Scouts." Officers claimed, with a bit of hyperbole, that if a stone were to be moved by a man, Yarkoni could detect it 100 years later and then follow the trail of the man who had moved it.

The shepherd served as an officer in the Israeli army from 1948 until 1969. Most of his exploits are still classified state secrets. We do know that he earned a *Tsalash,* or Israel's highest medal of honor, on three different occasions: this is an award that is so difficult to earn that it is frequently only conferred posthumously on the recipient. In 1959, the shepherd lost his left arm when wounded in action. Then in 1964 his leg was amputated after he was shot. He is buried in a Tel Aviv Israeli military cemetery.

*   *   *   *

The urology ward in any hospital is like something out of Dante. A filthy and depressing place. There are puddles of blood and urine everywhere. Miserable people, mostly old men, drag themselves about, pulling the rolling poles that hold intravenous and other bags connected to tubes running in and out of their bodies. They wander about, making little effort to keep the backs of their hospital gowns closed. Indifferent to their anatomical exposure.

A nurse stops by to check my temperature. "You need any more morphine?" she asks. "You think all Americans are drug addicts," I answer.

In morning prayers, the Jewish male thanks God for having made him a man. But looking around this ward of male misery, it is hard to see what males have to be grateful for. The average patient age is perhaps 70, but there are the occasional younger men, almost all with problems involving kidney stones, one only 27 years old. At the entrance to the ward, the doctors – in a bit of macabre humor – have constructed a window exhibit of kidney stones they have removed. The stones vary in color, texture and size, from small grains to something the size of a hawk egg.

In the room next to me is someone I have nicknamed Laptop Man. He has the usual bags and tubes, but also some sort of high-tech monitor on the top of his rolling pole that strikes me as resembling a laptop computer. He groans as he drags himself down the hall, pulling his rolling "laptop." He is a hospital parody of the yuppies in Orange County, rushing to catch their commuter flights to San Jose and Silicon Valley, dragging their laptops along.

* * * *

He was born in Siberia in 1886 and spent his first 13 years there in the tundra. His family then moved to Vilna, the capital of Lithuania. There Alexander Zaid joined the underground Zionist youth organizations, and at the age of 18 moved to Palestine. He worked in assorted jobs in different parts of the country. But he quickly discovered that his skills and his destiny lay in serving as an armed guardsman. The Jews of Ottoman Palestine were totally unarmed and at the mercies of every thief, hooligan and brigand.

In 1907 he initiated the creation of the very first militia of Jewish armed guardsmen in the Land of Israel since the time of the Romans. They would guard the fields and vineyards of Jewish farmers from predators and deter attacks on Jewish settlements. From this modest beginning would ultimately develop the Hagana and then the Israeli Defense Forces. The Watchmen, as they called themselves, dressed in Bedouin garb, with flowing *kafiya* headdresses, and lived on the land.

Zaid led the Watchmen stationed at the furthest frontier positions in the Upper Galilee when they came under ferocious organized attack by large bands of Arabs in 1920. The attack began innocently enough. The Arabs claimed they were chasing French soldiers, against whom they were rebelling in Lebanon, and asked to come into the fortified grounds of the Jews at Tel Hai. They were admitted in friendship, but once inside, drew weapons and the shooting began.

Zaid's comrade and one of the commanders in the fort was Joseph Trumpeldor, born in the Caucasus mountains. Trumpeldor had been the very first Jewish senior officer in the Czar's army and had fought heroically against the Japanese in the 1905 Pacific War, where he lost his arm. He dreamed of leading a Jewish army that would drive out the Turks from Palestine. Trumpeldor was killed in the battle at Tel Hai. Zaid survived.

Zaid organized irregular units around the country. He himself was wounded repeatedly in clashes with Arabs. By the 1930s, the Watchmen units banded together to form the Hagana, the Jewish national militia in Palestine, and a centralized command was established.

In the mid-1930s Zaid moved to a hilltop in what is now Tivon, to the east of Haifa. The Jewish National Fund had purchased tracts of land in the area and he served as their guardsman. He lived there on his own, the only Jew in the region. He established cordial ties with the Bedouin in the area and especially with the Saadiya.

In 1936, violence broke out and the Butcher's men went on a killing spree throughout the Galilee. It was a major baptism of fire for his beloved militia units. One night in 1938, Zaid was murdered in an ambush near his home. The Hagana tracked his killers and killed them.

It was a pattern of violence that would repeat itself endlessly for decades.

*   *   *   *

While relations between Bedouin and Jews throughout the Galilee were generally cordial, nowhere were they as truly warm as those between the Saadiya and Kibbutz Allonim. The kibbutz was built on a hill not far from the Saadiya lands, a few weeks before the murder of Alexander Zaid. It was created under a lacuna in Ottoman law, still operating in British Palestine, according to which any "town" having a watchtower and a wall could not be dismembered or removed. The tower and wall for the kibbutz were constructed in a single day in 1938, and by the time Mandate officials came along, the new settlement was a *fait accompli*.

Among the founders of the kibbutz was Shmuel Admon, who served as a senior officer in the British military before and during World War II. Later Admon became the chief artillery officer for the Hagana. Fluent in Arabic, he had a special interest in, and rapport with, the Bedouin and made efforts to maintain the warmth between the Saadiya and the kibbutz. In the days of fighting and violence, the Saadiya and the kibbutzniks helped one another, warned one another of dangers, took in one another. They attended one another's weddings and holiday celebrations. Their parties featured strange mixes of the *hora*, the Jewish folkdance, and Arab *debka* dances.

Near the entrance to the kibbutz is a natural spring, called *Ain al-Matr* by the Bedouin. The spring is regarded by the Bedouin as having special powers, curing illness and helping women become pregnant. Jewish farmers and Bedouin tribesmen would regularly greet each other there.

Some of the Bedouin held jobs on the kibbutz, as shepherds, plowmen, guards. One day, a member of the Saadiya named 'Ali approached the kibbutz secretariat. He was in tears. His wife had died and he had a six-month old infant to care for. He had no one to look after the baby while he was at work.

In those days, children on the kibbutzim were raised communally, in special children's homes operated by the community. The kibbutzniks were fanatically protective of these. No one was allowed inside except those appointed as child care workers, and there was cut-throat competition among the kibbutz members for the jobs. No one from outside the kibbutz was allowed to attend school with the kibbutz children. Even ordinary kibbutz members were denied free access to the children's home.

But the kibbutz made an exception for 'Ali. He was invited to bring his baby to the children's home. The child could stay on as one of the kibbutz children for as long as he wished.

*   *   *   *

In 1941 the Butcher returned to Baghdad, even more ferociously anti-British than he had earlier been anti-French. Like many Arab nationalists in Iraq, he identified openly and completely with the Nazis, and when a pro-German revolt was launched by Iraqi Arab officers in 1941, he joined with enthusiasm.

After being wounded badly, the Butcher was taken to Nazi Germany itself for treatment and training, where he awaited the end of the War. There he married a German woman. Wanted by the British, he tried to infiltrate back into the Middle East and hopped a flight from Europe to Cairo. The plane however was diverted to Tel Aviv airport, still under British Mandatory control, due to bad weather. A British officer and a Hagana Jewish soldier checked the passengers, but failed to recognize the man chatting with his wife in German as al-Kaukji.

After arriving in Cairo, he made his way to Syria. The Syrians decided he was the perfect commander for the Arab Liberation Army they were organizing, an army that would exterminate the Jewish infidels the moment the British colonial forces finally quit Palestine. Al-Kaukji was sent back to the Galilee, where he had fought against the British and the Jews ten years earlier.

The Jews were preparing to declare their own state, and al-Kaukji was placed at the head of the army militia of Syrian and Palestinian Arab fighters in the Galilee, the Jeish al-Inqaath. Syria hoped to use him as an instrument to annex all of northen Palestine, which it considered (and still considers) nothing more than Southern Syria.

Unlike many of the militia leaders fighting against the Jews, al-Kaukji had real military experience. He was nicknamed the Lion of Damascus.

*   *   *   *

When the War of Independence broke out in 1948, there was fighting in the vicinity of the Saadiya Quarter. The Saadiya had decided they wanted nothing to do with al-Kaukji's barbarians and refused to join them in their war against the Jews. The Butcher regarded the Saadiya as traitors, engaged in friendship and working with the infidel.

But the fighting between al-Kaukji's people and the Hagana

was getting uncomfortably close. One day, the Hagana fired in the direction of the Saadiya encampment from a nearby settlement, Shaar Amakim. No one was hurt, but many in the clan wanted to put distance between themselves and the battlegrounds. They fled to Galilean Bethlehem, still home to the last of the German Templars, most of whom had been expelled by the British during World War II due to their suspected Nazi sympathies.

Bethlehem was now in the hands of al-Kaukji's men. The nearby Templar colony of Waldheim had already been conquered by the Hagana, and so the battle lines lay in between. It was winter, early 1948. Al-Kaukji's men blocked the access road to Bethlehem with large boulders. The Butcher ordered the Germans removed to his rear, to the Galilee town of Zippori not far from Nazareth, which served as his command center. Most of the Saadiya also moved near Zippori, where they set up their tents. The Scout was with them.

*   *   *   *

One day some of the Butcher's men came through the camp asking for Salim Saadi. When they found the Scout, he was unarmed. He today insists that had his rifle been within reach, he would have finished off the gang on the spot. The militiamen asked him if he owns a rifle, and he said yes I have a hunting rifle. Good, they said, take us to it.

After seizing the weapon away from him, they took him into Zippori and locked him in the prison operated by the Butcher's men. He was beaten and interrogated. Among the militiamen stationed there were Arabs who had been under his supervision while working at Waldheim, the old Templar Colony. These were men who had resented taking orders from a youth back then and were now more than anxious to avenge the insult on their prisoner. They also knew that the Scout's family was on close terms with Jacob Salomon, the purchase agent for the Jewish National Fund and now a Hagana chief.

Salim was taken before the chief officer of the militia. The man started cursing him. You Saadiya, you who think you are noblemen. You were the rulers of this area under the Turks and under the British. And you are all spies for the Jews today.

Salim was kept in a prison cell for three days. He was fed some pita and dates. Among the officers in al-Kaukji's army was a man whom he had known in the days when both worked for the Templars. This militiaman was married to a woman from the Saadiya. While the others were distracted and preoccupied, the man approached the imprisoned Salim and whispered to him. The Butcher's people are planning to move you out to Syria tomorrow, where they plan to execute you.

But he had a plan. He would be the guard on duty outside the prison until 10:00 that night. During his guard shift, he would leave a window unlocked and slightly ajar. After he was relieved, the Scout could sneak out the window, but from that moment onward he would be utterly on his own. His friend would be under surveillance and unable to offer any further assistance.

At 10:00 the guard shift was relieved. The replacement was a huge hideous creature, fat and lazy with an offensive odor. This relief guard carried a powerful British musket. He spread out a huge mattress on the ground, ate an even larger meal, and by 10:30 was snoring as loud as a jackal.

The Scout silently pushed the window open and crept out, grabbing the blankets off the sleeping guard. In his rush, he neglected to steal the pig's rifle, an oversight that he regards to this day as one of the great mistakes of his life.

He found his way to the perimeter of the prison, which was a maze of razor wire and cactus. He tossed the blanket over the barbs, and crawled across it to safety.

He knew he was in mortal danger if he stayed in the territory of al-Kaukji. So he crossed the battle lines back into Jewish territory. He went to Kibbutz Allonim, where he was greeted warmly by his Jewish friends. They gave him scarce flour and he returned to the Saadiya Quarter.

He lived there alone in silence. All the others were away to the east, inside al-Kaukji territory. He spent his days walking the hills with his hunting rifle and bandolier, living off the land, helping himself to corn and grain from silent abandoned fields.

*　*　*　*

Hunting has always been his passion. He is a legendary hunter as well as a tracker. But he hunts for the challenge, for the sport. Since childhood, he has always been a strict vegetarian. No meat passes his lips. Not even fish. Today he only eats food that he has grown himself on his own lands.

For years he hunted with his beloved horse. Like himself, she was a pure-bred Arabian. She was a bit of a scout in her own right. When he slept in the field, if there were any strange noises nearby she would nudge him with her nose, shaking him awake. One day the horse was grazing when a poisonous snake bit her, a viper. He wept uncontrollably. He buried her in his fields.

*   *   *   *

One day he decided the time was ripe to bring his wife home. She and most of the others were living in shanties and tents inside al-Kaukji territory. Salim took his horse and rifle and set off. When he neared the village, he feared to enter, lest al-Kaukji's men identify him. Nearby he spotted an old charcoal seller named Hassan, referred to by all as The Negro. He asked The Negro to go into the village and speak to his wife, to let her know he had come for her.

But before The Negro could take his leave, four of the Butcher's militiamen suddenly spotted them. Who are you and what are you doing here, they demanded. Salim replied that he lived here. You see that shanty just over there? That is where I live. It is where I have always lived. Is this true, they asked The Negro. Of course it is, he swore. He has lived here for many years. The militiamen moved on. Salim retrieved his family and some other relatives, crossed back over the battle lines, and went home.

Some time later, his wife and their daughter went to stay with her parents. They were in al-Kaukji territory, back across the battle lines. The Hagana had pushed its lines forward, and had just taken Shfaram, but his in-laws were still on the wrong side of the battle lines.

The day after Shfaram was liberated by the Jews, Salim decided it was time once again to bring his family home. He borrowed three camels from a Bedouin herdsman, tied them behind his own horse, grabbed his rifle and set off. He had brought with him a letter of introduction from the kibbutz nearby, which served as an informal letter of transit. When he approached the front lines, an Arabic-speaking Iraqi Jew from the Hagana ordered him gruffly not to proceed.

A jeep drove up with Hagana officers. One of them, an officer from Acre, named Israel, knew Salim. He berated the Iraqi Jew for speaking disrespectfully to the Scout. But he warned Salim not to proceed because al-Kaukji's men were still in the area and would kill him without hesitation if they got hold of him. Salim insisted on taking his chances. Israel sent out word among all the Hagana fighters not to hinder him.

He proceeded first to Shfaram. There were fresh dead bodies lining the roads, reminders of the heavy fighting that had only just subsided there. In Shfaram all of the residents were indoors, not venturing outside due to fears of further fighting. Salim made his way to the police station, where the local Druse police commander knew him. The commander brought out food and ordered his men to bring feed for the animals. But he also urged his friend not to proceed, and instead to wait a few more days until the Hagana drove out the Butcher's men from the area where his wife was staying.

There were two Bedouin from the Saadiya being held in the Shfaram prison. Salim went to see the local Druse sheikh and asked him to release the Bedouin into his custody. The sheikh did so, and Salim took them home.

Three days later the Hagana drove the Butcher's army out of much of the Central Galilee. The battle lines had moved far to the east, past Zippori. The Saadiya were back under Israeli rule.

That evening the Scout was disturbed from his silent meditation. The entire clan suddenly materialized, returned home to their Quarter. His wife and children among them.

The war continued, but far from their tents.

*   *   *   *

The staff is worried about patients catching pneumonia. After surgery one breaths shallowly. Everything hurts and one just wants to lie on one's back. Perfect way to catch pneumonia. We are bullied into sitting positions by Jaris, an Arab male nurse, and told to stay that way as long as we can. My belly has more knife marks than that of an East Los Angeles gang-banger.

I get my first look at my neighbor. He had been brought in during the night with a 108° F fever, which is enough to kill a man half his age. He has some sort of kidney infection. He is thin and dark, in his 70s. Reminds me of Mahatma Gandhi. He has trouble speaking.

By mid-morning his wife has materialized. She is a tall woman, wearing traditional rural Arab garb. A dark skirt to the floor. A head scarf. She fusses about him and they speak in soft Arabic. He has an intravenous bag, like me, but she wants him to eat some solid food. He tries, but cannot hold it, and there is another round of choking and vomiting.

Later other family members come to visit him. They are Bedouin. From a small town half an hour away.

My youngest child was born in this same hospital. Obstetrics is the only part of any hospital where people smile. At the time, there was a young Bedouin peasant woman in the bed next to my wife. She had also just given birth to a boy. On the second day after delivery, she took the baby and painted his eyes and face with mascara. Some sort of Bedouin custom. The baby shrieked with outrage until the nurses rushed in to see what the emergency was.

*   *   *   *

The Talmud says that the nature of disease has evolved over the millenia. Disease originated when Man violated the commandments of God in the Garden of Eden regarding the Tree of Knowledge. The *Midrash* relates a legend according to which the origins of curing date from the time when the Children of Israel left Egypt in the Exodus. There were many diseased and disabled among the fleeing slaves. God thought it was unbecoming for them to be redeemed while suffering from afflictions and so sent the angel Malachi to administer cures to all.

Ah, but no sooner do they experience redemption than the fools build an idol, a golden calf, and bow down to it. In response, leprosy, deformities, and other afflictions returned to torment them.

At first, says the Talmud, disease of Man was different from its forms today. People would get sick when it was time for them to depart from the earth and the sickness was little more than a train whistle, telling them the time had arrived for them to get on board. It was only from the time of the Patriarch Jacob that things changed. Jacob became ill long before it was his time of death. Not as part of his exit, but as part of his life. Then later, during the period in which the Prophet Elisha – the disciple of Elijah – prophesized, some diseases developed for which cures could be offered.

Death in the Bible is regularly described as "gathering". Biblical figures do not die, they are "gathered" by God. Moses, Aaron, Jacob. The Great medieval Rabbi Shlomo Yitzhaki, known as Rashi, explains that at death, souls are simply returned by God to their storage areas, much the way someone would gather in laundry from the lines outside and bring it indoors, or the way one might gather up some crops from the garden and bring them indoors to protect them from the elements. The gathering at death is just bringing inside.

v. The War

BY THE 1940S, Sheikh Muhammed had passed on and his position at the head of the al-Heib tribe had been inherited by his son, known as Sheikh Abu-Yusuf. Relations between the Bedouin and their Jewish neighbors in Rosh Pina remained cordial. When violent pogroms broke out in the period of 1936–1939 throughout Palestine, the Bedouin did not lift a finger against their Jewish neighbors. In fact they were themselves targeted by the pogromchiks, the militiamen of the Butcher, al-Kaukji. Sheikh Abu-Yusuf had leased some land to the Jews on which they built a kibbutz in the Galilee, and – as a result – the Butcher's men issued a contract on his life.

Three years after the end of the European Holocaust, the United Nations passed the Partition Resolution, granting the Jews the right to establish a state in parts of Palestine. In 1948, they prepared for nationhood and for war.

Even before Israeli Independence was formally announced, Sheikh Abu-Yusuf approached the military commanders of the Jewish brigades. The Sheikh proposed a bond of blood. His tribe, the al-Heib, and the Jews would stand together, fight together, die together. It was not an act of expediency. The organized armies from five neighboring Arab states were preparing to invade the infant state of Israel. The Jews had only poorly-armed and poorly-disciplined militias. Their chances of survival seemed slim.

The Sheikh proposed that his fighters be integrated into the elite fighting militia of the Jewish Hagana, called the Palmach. Their unit would be called the Palheib, the al-Heib tribe of Bedouin fighters in the Palmach.[7]

*   *   *   *

In the winter of 1948, the Jews had not yet declared the Independence of their State. They were battling to hold on to the territories they controlled, under siege as Arab militias blocked roads and blockaded settlements and villages. Among the besiegers was the Butcher, al-Kaukji. One of the leaders of the Jewish community and a senior commander of the Palmach militia, Yigal Alon, was sent to the Galilee to organize military strategy. Plans to break the blockades, open the roads, and drive the Arab militias from the area were formulated as part of Operation Jephthah, named for the hero of misfortune, the military commander of the Book of Judges who came from the Gilead. Jephthah was the man who swore an oath too hastily to God and his foolishness ended up causing the sacrifice of his daughter.

The Palmach fighters expanded the theater of their operations and attacked the invading armies from Syria and Lebanon, in what became known as Operation Broomsweep. In these military operations, the Palmach units included Bedouin fighters and scouts. These were the first fighters in what developed into a long tradition of Bedouin serving in the military forces of the new Jewish state. While decorated and distinguished fighters in general, the Bedouin scouts in the army and police became particularly renowned throughout the country in the coming decades. In the police, they are identifiable by the special scout medallion on their uniforms. It is a silver eagle perched upon a rock and scouring the ground below.

*   *   *   *

The hours have passed and turned into a day, and then another. We are more alert now, awake for longer periods. Relatives pass in and out of the room all day, each set visiting its own survivor. Our wives spend

---

7   Source for description of role of the al-Heib in the war: Saul Dagan and Avner Kozviner, "Palheib: Bedouin in the Palmach in 1948," The Yigal Alon Center for the History of the Hagana Force, Yad Tabenkin, 1993 (Hebrew)

the days in the ward, fussing over us. "Where would we be without our wives," he says softly. "God makes men weak and women strong." Our wives chat among themselves, switching back and forth from broken Hebrew into broken Arabic.

His children are professionals of one sort or another. He tells me he has two sons in Europe, running businesses, one in Denmark and one in Italy. The son from Denmark calls the room and he is in tears.

Two of his grandchildren come by. The younger, a lovely eight-year-old girl named Maryam, kisses his hand and then holds his knuckles to her forehead, a common sign of respect and deference among Arabs. A small gesture that seems to capture everything about his family.

Language in Israel is a Babel of confusion, where people interchange languages seemingly at random, seeking out the best tongue of convenience for expressing any particular thought. Among pop singers in Israel, there are Jews who sing in Arabic and Arabs who sing in Hebrew. His family chats with him in soft Arabic, peppered with words and idioms in Hebrew, occasionally switching into Hebrew altogether.

Our families get to know one another, especially when their patients drift off. His wife reads Arabic women's magazines slowly. He refuses to eat the hospital food, and as a result my regard for him immediately shoots upwards ten points. His wife brings him food from home every morning and prepares him things throughout the day. He is a strict vegetarian and indeed eats nothing that was not grown on his own land by himself and his family.

We are feeling well enough now to joke. "I do not understand," he says. "Why is it that every person in this ward drags bags along behind him." The ward is populated with pathetic "bag men," dragging along assorted bags attached to hoses and pipes into and out of their bodies. Not necessarily passing through natural bodily openings. A urine bag at the end of a catheter. Intravenous bags. Drainage bags, into which tubes feed unidentifiable substances leaking from body wounds.

"It is the ticket people need to gain entrance," I explain. "When someone comes in and says Doctor, help me, I am dying, the doctor says never mind about that – do you have a bag?" We all roll with laughter, and in my case I have to hold my ribs tightly. The 12-inch incision is still fresh and there is real danger of turning the expression "side-splitting laughter" into something literal if I am not careful.

At one point I stand and walk towards the bathroom, but forget to take with me the drainage bag, still hooked onto a pole. After a few steps it beckons me back, and we all chuckle at the absurdity of the situation. "The dog forgets his own tail," I comment.

*   *   *   *

"I, the Lord, search the heart and test the kidneys,
in order to award all men according to their ways
and as fruit of their deeds."

– Jeremiah 17, 10

*   *   *   *

During the War of Independence, Haifa was a battleground with fierce Arab-Jewish fighting. The competition for the city was ferocious because it was the main port, and its control was essential for maintaining access to ships bringing in arms and immigrants. It was the last point in the country to be abandoned by departing British Mandatory troops. There were regular troops of the Transjordanian Arab Legion stationed in and around the city.

Jewish and Arab militias, composed of poorly trained irregulars, were scattered around the city. The handful of weapons possessed by the Jews were hidden in "slicks" or hiding places, some on the surrounding farms and kibbutzim. As war approached, the main Jewish militia, the Hagana, assigned a new commander to the Haifa front. He managed to assemble his entire militia of 150 men but then turned pale. The "fighters" included his high school Bible teacher and an assortment of middle-aged geezers, well past their prime. He asked how many of those present had ever fired a Bren machine gun. Only three had. Some of the others had actually had some practice firing a pistol.

The largest employers in the Haifa area were the port itself and the petroleum refinery, which had been built by the British to handle crude oil pumped in through a pipeline from Iraq. The pipeline had been one of the main targets for sabotaging by the Butcher's fighters in the 1930s. The refinery had been bombed and strafed by Italian fighters based in Libya during World War II. It employed a large workforce comprising both Arabs and Jews.

The stevedores of the port nearby were mostly Spanish-speaking Jews, immigrants from Saloniki in Greece, where they had dominated the longshoreman profession for generations. For centuries the port of Saloniki had been the only one on earth that shut down for the Jewish sabbath.

As the day of Independence for Israel approached, firefights broke out among Arabs and Jews in various locations in and around the city of Haifa. Arabs from Tira, a town just south of Haifa, conducted a number of raids, and in reprisal the Jews attacked the village, killed ten men, and blew up some houses.

In December, 1947, one of the militias of dissident Jews, operating outside the framework of the Hagana, threw some explosives at a crowd of Arabs outside the oil refinery. The Arab refinery workers set upon the Jewish workers, out-numbering them four to one. They murdered 39 Jews, and mutilated some of the bodies. Eleven others were seriously hurt.

Hagana headquarters decided there was no choice but to launch massive reprisals. Otherwise, the massacre would serve as precedent and incentive for further Arab atrocities. It mustered every fighter it could find in the area, 120 in all.

To the east of the city were two towns that were home to 800 Arab refinery workers. In their midst was the grave of one of the leaders of the anti-Jewish pogroms from the 1930s, later to become a shrine of pilgrimage for Palestinian suicide bombers from the Hamas terrorist group.

The decision was made by the Hagana command to retaliate there. The situation was tricky, as there were Transjordanian and British army units nearby. Orders were given to kill as many of the men in the villages as possible and to destroy property, but to spare all women and children. Among the Hagana squad commanders was a youth who would later become one of the country's leading economic professors.

The raid had the usual amount of bungling and snafus. Squads lost touch with one another and got lost. Weapons jammed when fed improper ammunition, as it was hard to find two rifles in Israel that used the same caliber of bullets. For many Hagana fighters, it was their baptism of fire. One of the commanders was the son of Alexander Zaid, the founder of the Watchmen. He had been seven when his father had been murdered. He later wrote about the Haifa battle, "There was pleasure in going out to battle, in applying what we had learned; there was no pleasure in killing."

Other battles took place in the city. The Jewish neighborhoods were mostly higher up the mountain slopes than the Arab neighborhoods. The Jews had no artillery, but designed "rolling shells," explosives set inside car tires and rolled down the slopes.

Before long the Battle of Haifa was over. Despite calls from the Jews that they lay down their arms and stay in their homes, almost the entire Moslem population fled the city for Lebanon, Syria and Transjordan. Most of the Arab Christian population stayed out of the fighting and stayed in their homes. They were to become an important and colorful part of the new city that grew and developed after the War.

*   *   *   *

Our Sages say in the *Midrash*: "Any person who makes himself merciful in a situation where he needs to be cruel will in the end be cruel in a situation where he should be merciful."

*   *   *   *

The Saadiya Quarter had emptied out completely during the battles. Many of the clan were now reluctant to return, because the area was under the control of the Jews. The Scout persuaded them to return and to stay. He had himself already returned to his home there, with his own family, and was on warm terms with the Jews. There was nothing to fear. His personal assurances prevented the abandonment of their lands by the Saadiya. His leadership was the key to the return of the tribesmen, to their joining the new State of Israel as citizens, this at the same time that so many others fled as refugees, fearing the vengeance of the Jews. Most of the families of those others who fled still live in Lebanon and Syria.

Under the new State of Israel, the nearby town of Tivon was built and populated with Jewish refugees arriving in the country. The Bedouin Quarter was renamed Basmat Tib'un, the Smile of Tivon, developing over time into a sister suburb. In Genesis, Basmat is the daughter of Ishmael.

*   *   *   *

Elsewhere in the country, relations between Jews and Bedouin varied. In the 1920s there had been only about 400 Jews and 20,000 Bedouin in the Negev area in the far south. Back in 1902, when the Ottomans were still in control, a Bedouin named Sheikh Salam Abu-Rabiya, speaking on behalf of several chieftains, approached the Zionist leadership with an offer of a Jewish-Bedouin alliance, aimed at wresting the country from the Turks. The Bedouin asked for arms and offered to acknowledge Jewish sovereignty in all of the biblical Land of Israel. Some of the Zionist leaders endorsed the idea with such enthusiasm that they urged young Jews to adopt Bedouin dress and life-styles.

Until the 1930s relations between Jew and Bedouin in the Negev were cordial. When a Bedouin encampment was destroyed in a desert flash flood, its Jewish neighbors rushed in with blankets and tents. But the Grand Mufti, the Moslem leading cleric in Jerusalem, was calling for war against the Jews, and a number of Bedouin clans and tribes enlisted in the campaign. Some of these sought annexation by the Saudis or by the Transjordanians.

Other Bedouin chiefs maintained their friendship with the Jews, including Sheikh Suleiman al-Hozail, who pitched his tents next to a Negev kibbutz, and Sheikh Abu Muamad, who lived near Revivim, the kibbutz in which Golda Meir lived. These friendly sheikhs later played a crucial role in providing intelligence services to the embattled

Negev Jews. It cut both ways. The Jews warned their Bedouin friends just before the Egyptian army invaded in 1948, and the Bedouin fled out of the path of war. The Bedouin did not forget the warnings.

During the War of Independence there were several armed clashes in the Negev between Bedouin and Jew, but even the Bedouin who opposed Israeli statehood tended to exercise moderation and restraint. The water pipeline from Gaza to the Negev was sabotaged by two Bedouin. At the same time, other Bedouin were employed as pipeline guardsmen.

*   *   *   *

His young grandson Salim and some other relatives are in the room when he weakly rises to walk to the bathroom. His wife helps him along. As he walks, the back of his hospital gown opens slightly, to his indifference. Young Salim catches a glance of a portion of his grandfather's bottom, and is having trouble controlling himself. He is both amused and embarrassed, and his face shows how desperately he is struggling to control his laughter at the absurd situation of being "mooned" by his own grandfather. His mirth is contagious; the rest of us in the room see his reaction and cannot control our own laughter. Two families rolling in senseless laughter amidst the misery.

"Salim," I wink, "next time don't forget your camera."

*   *   *   *

The Bedouin in the Palmach served as gatherers of intelligence on the enemy Arab armies. They showed great skill in sheep rustling, infiltrating enemy lines and returning with flocks for the besieged and starving Israelis. Almost as if they had a natural innate talent for such things. The Bedouin also infiltrated the neighboring Arab states, where they would climb telephone and telegraph poles and listen in to the talk.

There were occasional battlefront problems. In one battle, the Palmach unit was attacking a militia composed of fighters from a tribe with whom the al-Heib had long conducted a blood feud. The Palmach fighters found themselves in a poorly defended position and the Jewish commander ordered a retreat to better lines.

The Bedouin did not budge. Thinking perhaps they had not heard, the commander crawled to them and repeated the command. You do not understand, they explained. Those dogs have feared us for generations. If we move back now we will lose the deterrence and credibility it took us generations to build up. The commander was persuaded to make a stand from the current line, and to send several fighters around the enemy's flank. Ultimately it worked and the opponents fled the field.

When the Syrian army invaded the newly-declared State of Israel, it targeted the al-Heib tribe of Bedouin with particular ferocity. After all, these Bedouin were fighting alongside the infidel Jews. The Syrians sent infantry and armor to attack the Bedouin, and even dropped 50 kilogram bombs on them from planes.

Most of the Bedouin women and children under attack were evacuated to a nearby kibbutz. The wife of the Sheikh and a few other womenfolk stayed behind and carried ammunition and water to the defenders against the Syrians, Bedouin fighting alongside Jews. In one battle, the Sheikh's wife was hit by a Syrian bullet in her knee, and the Jewish medic tried to bandage it. She refused. That a man who was not her husband should look upon her leg was unthinkable. The Sheikh later prevailed upon her to submit to the indignity.

Ultimately the battle was decided and the Syrians driven off when a small two-inch mortar was brought into action by the Palmach. It was one of the few mortars in the entire Israeli arsenal at the time.

There was one important idiosyncrasy of the Bedouin fighters in the Palmach. While reluctantly wearing armored helmets, which never seem to be strapped on properly, the Bedouin soldiers drew the line when it came to boots. They went into battle barefoot.

*　*　*　*

Hussein Rahal al-Heib was from the same tribe. Born in Zarzeid in the Jezreel Valley, he served as an Israeli army scout for many years. He was a friend of the Shepherd, Amos Yarkoni, the Father of the Scouts. Eleven members of his family were killed in action while serving in the Israeli army.

In 1972 in a raid into Lebanon in retaliation for a terrorist attack on Israel, Hussein rescued an entire platoon of Israeli soldiers. They had entered a *wadi* that was heavily mined and where an ambush lay in waiting. From a distance he spotted the signs in the earth, and the platoon escaped unharmed. In another raid, he spotted a motionless rag lying upon the ground. He ordered the unit behind him to halt. Watch and you will see the rag come to life, he said. He tossed a stone near the rag. When the terrorist hiding in a foxhole beneath the rag leaped out, he was blown to pieces.[8]

---

8   Source: *Maariv,* April 26, 1996.

VI. The Clouds

"In a pillar of cloud will God speak."

– Psalms 99, 7

THE TALMUD explains what constitutes a "miracle" in the modern – which is to say the post-biblical – era. Miracles in the Bible had their own supernatural character, the sun suddenly stopping in the sky or the Red Sea parting. But such colossal tricks no longer occur. There is of course the miracle of the mundane, where babies are miraculously born and the seasons miraculously change. But this is simply the miraculous in everyday life.

Since the end of the biblical era, the Talmud tells us, miracles take the form of small variations in the natural order, things that could easily be "explained away" as natural phenomena. For example, a summer rainstorm in a place where such things rarely occur in the summer.

The clue is the timing. If the sudden, rare summer rainstorm occurs in the middle of a battle and saves an army from destruction, or if some other unusual natural event occurs right when you need it, then the timing suggests that something miraculous has occurred.

*   *   *   *

When the War was over, it was time to seek work. Many of the Saadiya were working on the lands of a wealthy Arab land-owner, an *effendi*, from nearby Itbin. They worked as guards for the fields. The Scout refused to join them. It was not dignified to be working there.

It was still in the days of National Emergency, in the first months after the birth of the new state. Everything was scarce and rationed. Most Israeli Arabs lived in areas under some form of military administration and supervision. The security situation everywhere was delicate. There was sabotage and infiltration.

To work, Salim needed to obtain a permit from the police. He went to the nearest police headquarters and applied. He was sent to a nearby quarry owned by a Syrian Jew named Damaski, the Man from Damascus. The workforce was largely Druse from the villages atop Mount Carmel. He walked to the quarry by foot each morning. But he disliked the work, which was filthy and demeaning.

He then applied for work at a small factory nearby owned by the Jew Klieger, in which cinder blocks were manufactured. They were used to put up simple housing and shanties for the masses of new immigrants flooding into the country. The work was more to his liking. Within weeks he persuaded the owner to hire away the members of the Saadiya who had been working as guards in Itbin, and the factory became a sort of family enclave.

While working there, he got a strange call one evening. It was from the new residents in the old Templar colony at Waldheim. The Templars were no longer there, having been expelled by the British and the Israelis for their Nazi sympathies. On the colony grounds a new agricultural experimentation center had been set up by the Jews. Researchers would study horticulture and seek the best strains of crops and animals to be raised by farmers in the country.

But the station had a serious problem. A hyena from Mount Carmel had learned of the existence of the farm animals at the station. It would steal into the farm every second night, like clockwork. It would kill a sheep and gorge itself, taking two days to digest the meat in full, then return for another kill. The station workers had tried to track and kill the hyena, with no success.

Many of those on the farm had heard of the legendary scout and his tracking skills. They sent a delegation to ask the Scout if he would help them. He agreed. He went to stay in the hut of Old Schreiber near the fields. He slept during the day, and prowled the fields at night. One night he walked silently and slowly across a field. From the corner of his eye he thought he sensed a slight motion. He stood in silence, staring into the darkness, and on the rock nearby he saw a slight trembling of an animal's ear. It was the hyena. He fired a single round into the chest of the beast. Hearing the gunfire, Old Schreiber came running.

The next day, photos of the dead hyena were in all the newspapers.

* * * *

King Solomon (or Suleiman) plays an important role not only in the Hebrew Bible, but also in the Koran and in Moslem legends. A Saudi legend tells of a King of Arabia who wrote to King Solomon complaining of a horrible sandstorm caused by an evil *djinn* or spirit. He asked Solomon for aid. King Solomon took his ring and called a servant to him, ordering him to buy an empty waterskin in the bazaar, take the ring and then to travel to Arabia with both.

The servant took the skin to the desert, where the Bedouin showed him the spot in which the storm blew its fiercest. He opened one end of the waterskin, held the royal ring in front of it, and into the skin the wind spirit was immediately sucked. The servant then placed the bundle on the back of his camel and returned with it to King Solomon's court.

King Solomon then took the wind spirit from the skin and commanded it to raise the large keystone to its appropriate place in the gate of the Temple that Solomon was in the process of building, thus completing the structure. Upon completion, a great feast was held in which the noblemen sat at a special table, but the scholars and teachers were seated at a golden table and were served the banquet by Solomon himself with his own hands.

* * * *

I have always had a fascination with tornadoes. I can understand those madmen who spend their vacations in the Oklahoma and Texas panhandles, chasing storms through Tornado Alley. I lived in the Midwest for several years, hoping to see one, but of course never did.

Strange swirling clouds always play an important role in the Bible. "Clouds of Honor" are said to hover over the Tabernacle in the

Wilderness, and they show the Israelites when the time has come to uproot camp and where to go in the desert. They also hold Pharaoh's army at bay while Moses prepares to lead the hordes through the Red Sea. They police the boundaries around Mount Sinai before God reveals Himself.

In the *Midrash*, the legends of biblical folklore, it is said that when two humans love one another, the vapors from their breaths join together in the air. According to a great *Chassidic* Rabbi, the Righteous One of Ruzhin, Aaron (the High Priest and brother of Moses) is said to have exuded such super-human quantities of love that his exhalations formed Clouds of Honor in the desert.

It is about eight months prior to the time when the tumor is discovered. On a Sabbath afternoon, my son calls me to the window. Look, there is a pretty cloud, he says. We see a dark funnel cloud, drifting below a larger cloud, positioned a few miles to our west over the Mediterranean Sea. The funnel extends perhaps 20% of the distance from the cloud to the ground.

It has been raining lightly on and off during the day. Not particularly stormy. It is October, the last weeks of summer and long before the serious rains begin. Just a short period after Yom Kippur.

We call the rest of the family over to the window and as we gaze, the funnel lengthens. It touches down. A true tornado. Technically, I guess it is a water spout, a tornado over water. It swirls darkly, moving slowly in the direction of our house, leaving the sea and moving up into the *wadi*, up the mountain, moving close to the Ahmadi Mosque. It no doubt lacks the power of the killers of the American plains, but hypnotizes us nevertheless. As it approaches our building, it lifts up, rising to the parental cloud above, into which it disappears.

A tornado in Israel is something virtually unheard of. I would have suspected that I imagined it or dreamed it, except that my family also saw it. And the following week an amateur film of it shot with someone's camcorder is on the TV news, albeit from an angle in which it is far less clear than what we saw out our window.

It was no dream.

Three weeks later, another day of passing storms. They come in off the Mediterranean, separated by episodes of calm breeze and sunshine. From the top of Mount Carmel one can watch them like passing trains.

As I watch, there is another tornado water spout. Again the kids see it with me. It is different from the first. Slender and narrow this time, gliding gracefully down to the sea. In almost the exact same position as the earlier one. It throws up a cloud of vapor and droplets where it touches the sea surface near the shore, which rises a few hundred feet into the air. Then it lifts up and disappears before it reaches the beach.

Computation of probabilities is part of my profession. I am an economist. (I heard you groaning.) Except that there are things whose probabilities cannot be computed or whose computations are meaningless. I do not believe there is a single father who holds his newborn child in his arms and looks into the baby's eyes and thinks, "Hmmm, there is a non-zero probability that the random collision and agglomeration of molecules could have created this very being."

What is the probability of *two* tornadoes materializing off the shore of a country in which tornadoes never occur, in the same spot and in the same season? What do these "pillars of cloud" mean? What do they foretell?

* * * *

"The water that Allah sends down from the cloud, then gives life with it to earth after its death… and the changing of the winds and the clouds made subservient between heaven and earth, these are signs for a people who understand."

– The Koran, Chapter 2, 164

* * * *

In the Bible perhaps the most dramatic story that occurs anywhere between Noah's Flood and the Exodus of the Israelites from slavery in Egypt is the *Akeda*, or the Binding of Isaac. Abraham takes his son and heir and binds him up, preparing to thrust the knife into him and sacrifice him to God. All at God's direct instruction.

Major surgery is in some ways similar to the Binding, the *Akeda*. One is held down helplessly, not by ropes but by anesthesia. The Man with the Knife prepares to thrust it into you. You do not know if you will emerge from the experience alive.

When Abraham binds Isaac, at the very last minute an angel intervenes to rescue the boy (actually already a mature adult). But when the original instruction was given to Abraham to bind and sacrifice Isaac, the Book of Genesis tells us that it came directly from God Himself, and not via some intermediary, not even through an Angel. To rescue someone from the necessity of going under the knife, a mere angel suffices. To agree to undergo the surgery in the first place, only a direct command from God – in person – suffices.

Both Abraham and Isaac submit to the command of the Binding without question. This from the same Abraham who "horse-trades" and argues God down from 50 innocents to 10, while trying to save Sodom and Gomorrah from their fates.

But Isaac is perhaps the real hero of the story. Ready to give up his own life to satisfy a commandment from God. However, he pays a wretched price for the experience. He is left a total emotional wreck. For the rest of his days in Genesis, he does almost nothing with his life. Digs a few wells, that is all.

He feels himself old and dying and calls in his two sons to him to receive their blessings, inheritances and birthrights. This is when wily Jacob hornswaggles Isaac, by passing himself off as Esau, the older twin. Isaac is so out of it that he lets himself get snookered.

Only one problem though. When Isaac calls in his sons before he dies to confer upon them their blessings, he is in fact *not* dying. He goes on and lives another forty years more. He only *feels* himself a human wreck.

This is what major surgery does.

*   *   *   *

"And all those who believe that He inspects kidneys,
and saves from death and redeems from destruction."

– From the Yom Kippur Prayers

*   *   *   *

In Jewish tradition it is believed that everyone's fate is decided for the coming year during its first ten days. In effect, everyone is on parole from the first day of the year in the religious calendar until the tenth, called Yom Kippur, the day of fasting, atonement, and introspection.

At the end of Yom Kippur, God makes an entry in His ledger, deciding who will live and who will die in the coming year. Human nature being what it is, most people do not take the ledger business too literally. It is too hard for people to grasp their own mortality or to believe their lives could be in the balance of anything.

All of medicine is a sort of scouting mission. All the more so for a cancer patient. One's entire anatomy is the object of search, evaluation, investigation, spying, eavesdropping. Each new test is a sort of Yom Kippur ledger, a page that will reveal if you will live or die in the coming year.

Meanwhile, you have no choice but to sit, bound in uncertainty, like Isaac, awaiting destiny.

* * * *

In the morning prayers, one of the first benedictions, part of the blessings on the Torah, is where a Jew thanks God for having granted his mind the capacity to distinguish between day and night.

I have always thought this a bizarre prayer of thanksgiving. How much smarts does it take to tell the difference between day and night? Every insect can do that, and indeed lots of plants. Why thank God for such an unremarkable capability? Isn't it almost like saying sarcastically, well thanks for nothing?

But it now makes sense. Every moment of my day is filled with uncertainty. Am I dying? Will I live to see next Yom Kippur? Is it day or night?

In preparation for the moment of accounting, Jews engage in special prayer services called *Selichos*, in which they beg God to forgive them for their sins. The *Selichos* prayers revolve around recitation of the Thirteen Attributes of God, and these are introduced by a plea to God to appear to us on earth in a cloud.

* * * *

Chassidism, that branch of Orthodox Judaism sometimes described as mystic, is traditionally divided into many different courts, often based around a charismatic leader, often named after the towns in Eastern Europe from which they originated. The Ruzhin *Chassidim* originated in a small town in the Ukraine. They had an unusual way of thinking about death.

In their view, one should expect humans to accept death with indifference, if not relief. A life is simply a period in which a soul occupies a borrowed body. Ordinarily when people use borrowed equipment or a borrowed book or vehicle, it is a relief for them to return it. It is a relief from pressure and responsibility. The happiest day in the course of a tour of duty in the Israeli reserves is when the soldier returns borrowed equipment. People returning rental vehicles at the airport usual breath a sigh of relief.

The Ruzhiners argue that humans should feel the same relief when they are released from their borrowed bodies. They return the rental property to its owner and it is no longer their responsibility. Moreover, when someone dies, in a sense it is a cause for celebration. This is because God has placed every person on earth to fulfill some function or other. If that person dies, this can only be a sign that he or she has completed the task assigned, carried out his or her purpose on earth with success, whatever that purpose was.

When someone dies at a young age, this is simply a manifestation of that soul having fulfilled the tasks it was assigned more rapidly and efficiently. When a righteous person dies, this is a special reason to celebrate, for an unusual set of feats must have been achieved and a special gift of benefits must have been conferred.

So why do humans fear death, ask the Ruzhiners? Well, it is simple. The soul fears that it has not yet successfully completed all the tasks it has been assigned for this life. It fears it will fail its Creator. And for this reason it fears death.

VII. The Spaniards

THE DETAILS of his mission are obscured in the mists of time. We know little about him. But he changed history.

In the year 710 AD, a Bedouin scout named Tarif was dispatched across the straits from Morocco into Gothic Spain. Sent with a small contingent of armed Arabs and Berbers, his mission was to explore the Iberian territories in preparation for their invasion and conquest. He is sometimes confused with the great general, Tarik, who actually led the invasion of Spain the following spring. But the general was a Berber, whereas the scout was an Arab.

The cape at the very southern tip of Spain is still called Tarifa, after him. Like the scouts sent to spy out Canaan in the Bible, he was sent by a Moses. *His* Moses was Musa (Arabic for Moses) ibn Nosseyr, the lord governor of North Africa, a man whose beard was always carefully dyed red, a direct appointee by the Caliph himself. The information Tarif collected and the ease and success of his mission convinced the lords of the African Maghreb that Spain was ripe for the picking. Musa saw Spain as the starting point of a new campaign that would allow him to fulfill his lifelong dream of preaching from the Koran at the Vatican in Rome.

Tarif led a small mixed force of North Africans, Moslems and Christians. It was only 91 years since the *hegira* of the Prophet, in the year 622 of the Christian calendar, when Mohammed left Mecca to establish the new religion in Medina. Ten years later, the Prophet had died and the Caliphate was established.

Ten years after that, the Arab governor of Egypt sent out the first expeditionary force to the West, conquering the territories that now form Libya. It was there that the Arabs had their first encounters with tribes of Berbers.

In the year 681 the first Arab scouts and raiding parties set eyes upon the Atlantic Ocean in the western part of Morocco. The Byzantine infidels had been driven from most of Africa. The Berber nomads were next in line for absorption by the expanding empire.

Berber resistance to the Arab conquerors was led by a warrior Queen named Kahina. It seems somewhat bizarre, but she and her tribesmen were Berber Jews. The Jews had lived among the Berbers since Roman times, generally on amicable terms. Some of the Berbers drew close to them in religion, including Kahina's own tribe in the Atlas mountains.[9] She led the resistance to the Arab invaders, but was defeated and killed. Thereafter the Berbers made their peace with the rule of the Arabs and most converted to Islam.

The unitary Arab regime in Africa was actually composed of a large variety of peoples, cultures and religions. City dwellers and nomads. Moslems, Christians, Jews, Greeks, Vandals, pagans.

*   *   *   *

At the tip of a peninsula in Morocco, just opposite Gibraltar and Spain, there was a small Christian dukedom ruled by one Julian, probably a Byzantine appointee. Following Gothic custom, he sent his daughter for schooling to southern Spain, where she was the ward of a Gothic King named Roderic in his palace in Toledo. The King however abused and ravished the girl. Her enraged father invited the local Arab overlord to form an alliance with him and help him avenge himself on Roderic and the Spaniards.

The alliance was sealed. The army was led by Tariq ibn Zayid, a Moslem Berber chief, governor of Tangier. He was accompanied by his female slave, Umm-Hakim. They stopped at an island during the crossing, where the beautiful slave girl was left behind to direct communications and logistics. The island was thereafter named for her.

Tariq led the invading force, which landed in 711 near the huge

---

9 "The Kahina: Legendary Material in the Accounts of the 'Jewish Berber Queen'." *The Magreb Review* 7 (5 & 6): 122–125, 1982.

granite mound guarding the straits from the Iberian side. The Spaniards had mistaken the arriving fleet for one composed of the usual merchant ships they were accustomed to seeing in the area.

The area across the straits from Morocco was known to the Arabs as the Land of the Vandals, one of the barbarian tribes that had plagued Rome. Arabic has no "V" sound and so the Arabs dropped the "V" in Vandalitia, as the Goths referred to it. Accordingly, the south of Spain was called by the Arabs Andalusia, and has been known as such ever since. A mountain is called *Jebbel* in Arabic and this granite mound by the straits became known as the *Jebbel* of Tariq after the invasion. In time, the name was modified to become Gibraltar.

Once the beachhead was secured, Tariq took nearby Cartagena, the old town established by the Punic refugees after the destruction of Carthage by the Roman legions. From there he marched on Cordova. According to the Arab historian ibn Abdel Hakim, after taking Cordova Tariq asked that a table be brought to him. A suitable table was found in a castle nearby. The table was covered with gold and jewels and was worth 200,000 dinars. The historian insists that the table had belonged to King Solomon himself in Jerusalem.

According to Abdel Hakim's history, along the way Tariq came upon a building with a large number of padlocks on its door. The locals explained that every new king added his own padlock and invited Tariq to add *his*. Tariq insisted first upon knowing the contents of the building. He broke down the door, and therein he found a room full of portraits of Arab warriors. This confirmed his own fulfillment of ancient prophecy. It had been foretold long before that when the door with the many locks would be opened, the people whose portraits were inside would conquer the country.

Tariq then led his force north until Toledo itself was taken in a huge battle against superior forces. The battle is known as the Victory in the Valley of Umm-Hakim, again named for the beautiful slave girl. The Christian Goths abandoned Toledo in panic. The Jews of Toledo welcomed the Moslems in euphoria as liberators from their Gothic tormentors.

*   *   *   *

The Arab Moorish forces overran Spain and invaded France. They terrified the Spaniards with their boulder-tossing ambuscades. They continued northwards until they reached Tours, not far from Paris. There they fought the Battle of Poitiers against the Franks. The historian Edward Gibbon remarked that had this battle been won by the Arabs, Oxford University would have been set up for circumcised students to study the Koran. As it turned out though, the Franks were victorious. They were led by Charles Martel.

Martel was actually his nickname, meaning "hammer." A thousand years earlier, the leaders of the Jewish warriors who evicted the Greek Seleucid pagans from Jerusalem had also called themselves The Hammers. In their language this was Maccabee and those warriors are the heroes of Hanukah.

Like so much else, the struggle of the Maccabees began from the kidneys. In the Book of Maccabees, an external or apocryphal book (once included as a Book of the Bible in its Greek form but later dropped), it is told how their military campaign began. A man tried to perform a pagan ritual at an altar near Jerusalem in obedience to the pagan king. The Book tells of the reaction of Mattathias, the father of the Maccabee brothers: "When Mattathias saw this thing, he was inflamed with zeal and his kidneys trembled, neither could he forbear to show his anger according to judgment: wherefore he ran, and slew him upon the altar."

Hanukah began from the kidneys.

*   *   *   *

While defeated in France, Spain became a multicultural jewel, a pinnacle of world civilization, remaining at least partially under Arab rule until the eve of the first voyage of Christopher Columbus. At the very limits of the known world, far from the administrative capitals in Damascus and Baghdad, Spain became the center of world learning, science, medicine, mathematics, and poetry.

It was the destination of choice for the scholars from the infant universities of Sorbonne and Oxford, who came to glean knowledge. Many a Catholic monk came to Spain to study the scientific and philosophical writings of ancient Greek pagans, works that had only been translated into Arabic and Hebrew. At times, the writings would be taken back to the lands of Christendom, where other Jews would translate them into Latin. In this way, the West imbibed its own Western Greco-Roman intellectual roots by way of the Arabs and the Jews.

For Spanish Jews this was the Golden Era, a New Jerusalem, and Arab Spain for them represented not only unprecedented economic prosperity but also social acceptance and rabbinic scholarship. Spain replaced Iraq as the scholarly capital of Judaism. Arab Spain had Jewish cabinet ministers and diplomats, besides the *de rigueur* court physicians. One even conducted correspondence with the distant Turkic Kingdom of the Khazars beyond the Caucasus mountains, whose ruling classes had recently converted to Judaism. Spain produced the world's leading rabbis and Jewish philosophers, including Maimonides.

A book on theology entitled "The Fountain of Life" was originally written in Arabic, then used for centuries in Latin translation as a standard basic text among educated Christians throughout Europe. Its author was one Avicebron, a presumed Catholic monk. It was only in 1850 that it was discovered that this "Christian" theologian, the man who had instructed so many generations of Christian students and intellectuals, was in fact the Spanish rabbi and poet Solomon ibn Gabirol, whose name had been corrupted into Avicebron. The "Christian" philosopher Avicebron was expelled from Spain after the Inquisition and Reconquista, together with all of the other Spanish Jews.

In Arab Spain, Jew, Christian and Moslem generally lived together in harmony, at least until the Almoravid and Almohad invasions from Morocco triggered an era of Iberian violence, intolerance and persecution. In the same year in which Columbus was dispatched to cross the Atlantic, the Jews were finally expelled altogether from Spain. Columbus navigated the journey using the maps of a Spanish Jew. The very first European left behind as a settler in the New World by the Explorer was a Spanish Jewish refugee who had accompanied him, Luis de Torres.

*　*　*　*

There have been quite a few rabbis with Arab names. In the Talmud, one of the more important Rabbis was named Ishmael. He is best known for enumerating the Thirteen Logic Principles through which the Laws of God and the Talmud are to be studied. Rabbi Saadiya was the last of the great scholars of Babylon. After his death the center of gravity for Jewish life shifted to Arab Spain. Several important Rabbis had names that began with the Arabic "ibn", meaning "son of", such as Moses ibn Ezra from Granada and Salomon ibn Gabirol from Tudela.

*   *   *   *

Suleiman is Arabic for Solomon. Rabbi Suleiman was a Spanish Jew who left his home in Fez, Morocco, and moved to the Galilee in the 16th century to become one of the students of the great ARI (the Lion). The ARI was Rabbi Isaac Luria, the master of Jewish mysticism in the town of Safed in the Galilee, one of the four traditional Jewish holy cities in the Land of Israel. Suleiman worked there as a scribe, copying Torah scrolls and other sacred documents.

There is one unique Torah scroll that he copied, which has always been said to have mysterious qualities. It sits today in the ark of the Abuhav synagogue in Safed, near the synagogue of the ARI. A Torah scroll may only be used in worship if every single letter in it is correct and perfect. Rabbi Suleiman's scroll contains several letters that are incorrect, that run into one another, and so the scroll cannot be used during worship. Except that three times a year on Jewish holy days, the letters are said to rearrange themselves, correcting themselves mysteriously, making the scroll valid and so the worshippers read from it. But only on these holidays. Old-timers in the synagogue insist that in the 1950s a skeptic opened the Suleiman Torah scroll on a weekday to check out the legend; he took sick and died within days.

Rabbi Suleiman lived out his life in Safed, and began a dynasty of Spanish-tradition rabbis. In each generation, his descendents would spend part of their lives studying the sacred books in Jerusalem and Safed, and part in service to some Jewish community somewhere in the world outside of Palestine.

*   *   *   *

Many generations later, there was a descendent of Rabbi Suleiman named Rabbi Nissim, born in Algeria in 1882 when his own father, coincidentally also named Suleiman (after his 16th century ancestor), was in service there as a rabbi. Like his ancestors, his mother tongue was Medieval Spanish, or Ladino, still spoken by the Spanish Jews centuries after being expelled from Spain. Rabbi Nissim studied Talmud in Jerusalem from the age of six, was ordained as rabbi, and married in the ancient Yohanan Ben-Zakai synagogue inside the walls of the Old City of Jerusalem. Throughout his life he served overseas Jewish communities, including the Jews on the island of Malta.

When World War I broke out he was the rabbi for a congregation of Spanish Jews from Syria in New York City. He gathered his family and attempted to return to Palestine, which was a battleground in the war. Most of his kin were living in Jerusalem, inside the Old City and not far from the Western Wall.

The Turkish authorities however would not allow him to enter. The vestige of the Ottoman Empire was at war with France. Rabbi Nissim was travelling on French papers, having been born in French Algeria, and so was regarded as an enemy alien. Instead, he took a series of rabbinic posts in Egypt, and moved with his family to Haifa in 1947, shortly before the State of Israel came into existence.

Before World War I, Rabbi Nissim served for several years as the rabbi for the Jews in Gaza City. This was decades before Gaza became a cesspool of hatred and violence. At the time, the Jews and Moslems of Gaza City enjoyed the most cordial of relations. In particular, Rabbi Nissim was on intimate terms with the Moslem Mufti or religious leader of Gaza. The two engaged in long theological discourses. Rabbi Nissim was a scholar not only of Jewish religious sources but also of the Koran and the Christian New Testament. Sometimes when a Moslem would approach the Mufti with a difficult religious question, he would talk it out with Rabbi Nissim before issuing a pronouncement.

*   *   *   *

When the great Jerusalem Righteous Man, Rabbi Arie Levin, took his wife to a physician with sharp pains in her leg, he began the interview by saying to the doctor, "We are feeling pain in my wife's leg."[10]

When a couple lives in harmony, they have only one body.

*   *   *   *

The number seven always plays a strange, mysterious role in the Bible. Time is based on the seven-day week. The Temple operates around a seven-arm candelabra. The Bible is sprinkled with sevens.

Seven sevens, or 49, is an even more mysterious number. It is the number of days to be counted ritually from Passover, when the Israelites fled from Pharaoh, until the holiday of the Granting of the Law, the day on which God revealed Himself to the Israelites at Mount Sinai.

Seven sevens are also the cycle of human events as spelled out in Leviticus. Land contracts, leases, debts and indentures all last only until the end of each 49 year cycle. Every 49 years, there is a rebirth. The land, humans, life start all over. Trumpets sound and the jubilee year is proclaimed, when we are commanded to proclaim liberty throughout the land unto all the inhabitants thereof. If that sounds familiar, it may be because that is what is inscribed on the Liberty Bell in Philadelphia.

It has been 49 years since my birth in Philadelphia, a few miles from the Liberty Bell, when the cancer is discovered. If I survive, it will be to begin a new cycle. After the trumpet. After my jubilee year.

*   *   *   *

Yitzhak Netser was born in a kibbutz in 1948, just a few days before the United Nations voted to partition Palestine and to allow the creation of the State of Israel. From his early youth he was on intimate terms with the Bedouin who lived nearby. He spent time with them, learned their language and life style. As a 19-year-old soldier he was killed in action in 1967. His family then donated funds to hold

---

10 "Thoughts about Genesis," Prof. Yeshayahu Yarnitsky.

annual memorial conferences and essay contests with the Bedouin as the subject.

In 1971, a Bedouin sheikh named Musa Al-Ataouna gave a talk at one of these conferences.[11] He described the long history of friendship between his tribe and that of the early Jewish pioneers in the Negev near Gaza. During his talk, he recalled having heard of the intimacies between the Mufti of Gaza and a learned Jew named Alkayam. He said that many Moslems came to consult the Jew about the contents of the Koran, because he was as well-versed in the Koran as were the Moslem scholars from Cairo, and they regarded him as a judge. He was on especially warm terms with the Al-Ataouna Bedouin.

"Alkayam" was not the correct last name of Rabbi Nissim, although it is not too far off. The sheikh apparently recalled the name of the learned Gaza scholar in muddled form after many years.

The al-Ataouna tribe were the first Negev Bedouin to engage in land transactions with the Jewish pioneers, and sold them the land for Kibbutz Ruhama, located in what had earlier been known by the Bedouin as the *Jamama*. The Turkish Authorities however refused to acknowledge the lands as having belonged to the Bedouin, and only when the Rabbi of Istanbul intervened with the Ottoman government was the transaction recorded as completed.

The Bedouin from the al-Ataouna tribe maintained warm relations with the kibbutz farmers and protected them from brigands. When thieves made off with the kibbutz horses, the Bedouin tracked them down and forced them to return the booty. When the NILI network of spies working for Great Britain's General Allenby operated in Ottoman Palestine, helping the British drive out the Turks during World War I, they were hidden and abetted by Kibbutz Ruchama and its Bedouin friends.

Rabbi Nissim was the Alkayam of Gaza of whom the Bedouin sheikh spoke. Many years later the granddaughter of Rabbi Nissim met an eccentric American on a Haifa university campus, married him a few months later, and we have three children together.

* * * *

11 His talk appears in Yaakov Aini and Ezra Orion, *The Bedouin,* Institute for Desert Research, Ben-Gurion University, Beer Sheba, 1988 (Hebrew).

In one of the Taifa Spanish states, the Moslem ruler took a Christian princess as bride from a land to the north. They built together a life of love, but she pined for her homeland, its cold weather and its fields of snow.

The Prophet Mohammed said that marriage is one half of religion. Her Moslem lord and husband decided to bring the snow to her. One night, while she slept, he surrounded the palace with newly planted almond trees, full of white blossoms. When his bride awoke, she found that her new home was surrounded by "snow".

VIII. The Hunter

SCOUTS IN THE BIBLE were sometimes in a politically delicate position. One day the King of the Ammonites, the nation-city in Transjordan located in what is today Amman, passed away. He had helped King David long before he was king, when he was but a refugee in the wilderness being hunted down by King Saul. When the Jordanian King died, David – now the most powerful ruler in the region – sent a delegation to pay his respects to the mourning royal family of the neighboring kingdom.

But the princes in the kingdom distrusted David's intentions. He had grown too powerful. His delegation was regarded by them as a group of spies. They were suspected of coming for the purpose of scouting out the city and discovering its weak points. The hosts seized the Israelite delegates and humiliated them by shaving off exactly one half of the beard of each man, while tearing apart his clothes. So disgraced, they were sent back to report to King David.

He avenged them militarily soon after.

* * * *

Salim's reputation as a legendary tracker turned out to be a mixed blessing. One day in 1952 he received a paper ordering him to report for duty to the nearby police headquarters. The police in the country were desperate. They needed scouts and trackers. The borders of the country were being infiltrated. And there were thieves everywhere. The police were at a loss. There were few, if any, with his training and talents. He was being conscripted to serve the new State of Israel.

Forget it, he said. He had a wife and three children. He fled and hid from the police for 15 days, unable even to notify his employer where he was or what was going on. But, like the time he had run away from home as a child, he was soon found out. Two policeman handed him a writ ordering him to report for duty.

He was shipped off to the national police induction center in Jerusalem. There he was fitted with an awkward police uniform and a floppy hat. The uniform did not fit and kept slipping off the infuriated young man. He was so annoyed on the day of the induction that he refused to eat anything at all. By evening he was in the police compound in Rehovot, south of Tel Aviv.

His first night as a policeman ended suddenly and unexpectedly at 4:00 AM. He was awoken by the duty officer. Two milk cows had been stolen from a nearby farm. He was assigned to track them. He agreed, but on condition that he be excused from wearing the intolerable policeman's uniform. It was his very first official police case.

The Scout had never been in this part of the country before. He did not know the terrain. Moreover, the ground was largely loose sand, which made it more difficult to detect tracks.

He led the hunt. But after a few hours he was faint from hunger. He had not eaten in well over a day. He asked the others to bring him some pita bread and an onion bulb.

Late in the afternoon, he had tracked the stolen cows to a grove of trees not far from the sea. The cows could be seen from a distance, grazing quietly among the trees. But this was the most dangerous part of the hunt. The thieves could be hiding nearby in ambush and were no doubt armed. He carried only a small service revolver. He told the other policemen to stay back while he investigated. He discovered that the area around the cows was clean and the grove held no surprises. The thieves had fled.

Shortly thereafter the cows were returned to their owner. The owner asked to present the Scout with a modest reward, a token of his appreciation. The Scout refused. He would never accept anything for his work from anyone, beyond his modest policeman's salary.

*   *   *   *

Our bodies contain tiny Bedouin scouts known as antibodies. They

are skilled trackers. They follow the trails of infiltrators and exterminate them.

But unlike the human-size scouts, these tiny scouts sometimes
fail. They lose a trail or fail to follow tracks or confuse the quarry
being tracked for something else. Among the conditions that can
result is cancer.

Having cancer is a lot like the Oscars ceremony. Week by week
one does assorted medical tests, returning a few days later to get the
results. There are notes inside little sealed envelopes. One opens the
envelopes to see who the surprise winner is, Life or the Angel of
Death.

*   *   *   *

Jacob Salomon had served as the land procurement agent who first
established ties of friendship with the Saadiya. By the 1940s he had
become a wealthy and eminent attorney in Haifa, and had built one
of the country's largest cattle ranches south of the city.

When the War of Independence broke out in 1948, Haifa was
the scene of harsh Jewish-Arab fighting. The Arabs brought in large
numbers of volunteer fighters from neighboring countries, setting up
strongholds in the Arab neighborhoods throughout the city. Salomon
was a leader in the Jewish militia, the Hagana, and served as political
liaison.

The Hagana proved the stronger military organization and by
April 1948 had seized control of the entire city. The mayor of the city,
Shabbtai Levy, convened an assembly of Jews and Arabs in the Haifa
City Hall, a stone building overlooking the port, to try to restore
peace and order.

The Hagana was represented by Salomon. The lawyer/rancher
pleaded with the local Arab leaders to urge the Arab residents of Haifa
to stay put and not obey the orders they were receiving from the Arab
Higher Committee, the Palestinian official leadership, to abandon the
city.[12] Salomon assured the Arab delegates that no Arabs would be

12 A description of the events and the role of Salomon appears in an article by historian
Efraim Karsh in *Commentary*, July–August, 2000, pp. 32–34.

harmed if they remained in Haifa and under Israeli jurisdiction. The Hagana and the Jewish national leadership were issuing similar calls to the Haifa Arabs to remain in their homes. Most ignored the calls and joined the masses of refugees fleeing the newly-formed Jewish state.

After the war ended, the attorney Salomon expanded both his law practice and his cattle ranch. He hired Mahmoud Saadi, the brother of the Scout Salim, as his top hand and as his cattle buyer. Mahmoud had worked in a variety of jobs, including some with newly arrived Jewish refugees living in squalid transit camps near Haifa. As part of these jobs, he had picked up Yiddish, the language of the Jews from Eastern Europe, a mixture of German and Hebrew. He may be the only Yiddish-speaking Bedouin in the world.

Salomon, who had been a close friend of his father, relied on Mahmoud's judgement in buying cattle and entrusted him with large sums of cash for procurement. But at one point Mahmoud became restless and spoke of going to Texas, where the world's greatest cattle ranches operated, perhaps using his expertise to become a cattle buyer out there, amidst the sage and the blue bonnets.

The lawyer made a suggestion: why not stay and become an associate member in the Egged bus cooperative? Egged was the largest economic cooperative in the world, as well as being a well-financed monopoly. It had turned bus driving into a high-prestige and highly-paid profession, especially for associates, who were regarded as being among the patricians of the new socialist state.

Mahmoud went to the Egged offices in Haifa and applied for membership. But he was turned down peremptorily. Egged was dominated by the doctrine of socialist monopolization of economic power, popular at the time in Israel, promoted by the labor leaders who controlled the governing party and the cabinet. It was an ideology based on Jewish labor, the insistence that Jews should refrain from becoming employers of Arabs and should perform all productive and demeaning occupations themselves.

While sounding noble, the implications of this doctrine were often socialist discrimination. Egged was not admitting any Arab associates, with only a handful of exceptions. The exceptions were

Arabs who owned their own buses and had already operated some established bus route before the creation of the State. *They* were welcomed as members; cynics would say it was to protect Egged's monopoly.

Mahmoud related the story of his rejection to the lawyer Salomon. Next day, the latter stormed into the Egged office and, within moments, not only was Mahmoud a full Egged associate, but his buying-in fee, the equivalent of a taxi medallion in New York City, was a third of the normal level. Mahmoud became the first Bedouin associate member of Egged.

* * * *

The weeks went by. Salim only rarely managed to get away from police work to visit with his family, whom he had left back home on his land. Four days off each month were all he was permitted. One day, his family was considering hiring a caretaker for the 100 or so head of cattle they kept on their land. The Scout wanted to oversee and to check up on things back home.

The duty officer at the police station was a friend, an Arabic-speaking Iraqi Jew. The Scout explained the problem, and the officer listed him as "present and accounted for," even after he sneaked out and took the bus home. When the bus reached Central Haifa, it was raining and the last bus of the day to his village had already left. He ran across a bus driver in the station he knew and explained the problem. The driver took him to Tivon, the town nearest his home, and he walked the rest of the way by foot. He arrived home soaking wet and exhausted. The next day he had to rise before dawn to make it back to the station before he was listed as AWOL.

* * * *

In the summer of 1952, he was stationed south of Jerusalem at the Beit Shemesh police headquarters. One day two Jewish soldiers were reported missing. The Scout followed their tracks until the bodies were discovered. The two had been out on a patrol, but had decided to take a nap in a grove of trees. While sleeping, they had been stabbed to death.

The Scout followed the trail of the murderers. It led down into a dry wadi, and from there toward the Jordanian border. He climbed down into the wadi to follow the tracks but when he reached the bottom, there was a hail of bullets all around, gunfire directed at him from Jordanian territory. He jumped toward the far side of the gully, where he would be out of their line of fire. Meanwhile, Israeli army troops returned fire at the Jordanian troops. In the commotion, the Scout hiked to the west for two kilometers to a spot where he could emerge safely.

In 1953 he was transferred to the Ashkelon police headquarters. One summer night a flour factory and warehouse in the downtown was burglarized. He was called to the scene. He identified the thief's footprints in the flour dust on the factory floor. From there, he went with some other policemen to an alley where the local thieves were known to congregate.

He walked through the alley, glancing at the shoes of the people sipping coffee there. This is the one, he said and pointed. The police grabbed the man, who insisted he was innocent. They took him to his shanty, where they found the stolen flour and crates of stolen factory machine parts.

*   *   *   *

Next to the Ashkelon courthouse lived an old man who raised ducks and chickens in his yard. One day thieves broke into his pen after midnight and stole the animals. The police were called, but were unsure whether to call out the Scout. After all, the earth around the yard was covered with asphalt, nothing but sidewalks and streets. What good would it do? What could a tracker find?

The Scout arrived anyway. He pointed to footprints made from the summer dew, visible on the asphalt. He tracked the prints to a field behind a gas station, where some canvas sacks had been stashed. The Scout took cover and waited. Before long a man appeared on a bicycle with a crate strapped to its rear. Salim stepped out and told the man he was under arrest. But he was out of uniform and the thief tried to make a break. The Scout drew his pistol and showed a police ID. The thief was arrested. Later that day his accomplice was apprehended.

South of the city, a band of thieves stole a stack of expensive aluminum irrigation pipes. The Scout was called to investigate. But things looked fishy. There was a team of Druse night guardsmen on duty, who were supposed to patrol the fields and guard against thefts. When the night guards were interviewed, they insisted they had been off in a distant field, two kilometers away. But near the spot from which the pipes had been stolen were cigarette butts and signs in the sand. Everything pointed towards the guardsmen having been in cahoots with the thieves, having taken a payoff to turn a blind eye while the pipes were stolen. When confronted with the evidence, they confessed.

*   *   *   *

The Chassidic rabbi, the Maggid of Mazeritch, would say that pain and suffering should not be regarded by man as evil, because God does not inflict evil on man. Instead, man should regard them as bitterness, not evil. Bitter, like the taste of medicines, needed to attain health.

When the famous Rabbi Moshe-Leib was terminally ill and suffering from extreme pains, he would begin his prayers by saying, "Now, pains, be off with you while I pray." When he would finish, he would say, "Okay pains, you may return now and continue your purpose."

*   *   *   *

It was Saturday. Some thieves had stolen a cow and mule from a farm in the Negev. The police came to investigate. But the commander was reluctant to pursue them. It was the Sabbath, and besides there was nothing but sand dunes all around, sand blown by the wind, in which it was hopeless to find tracks. In any case the thieves were no doubt over the border by now.

The Scout insisted on pursuit. From the tracks and signs he could tell the thieves had not crossed the border into Egyptian territory yet, and so were still on the loose inside Israel. He trudged across the dunes alone with a rifle. Eventually he saw some movement behind a dune and knew he had found them. But he was alone and – as always – his job was to locate the perpetrators, not to apprehend them. He needed to call in the backup.

He returned to the road and the waiting police vans. It had been three hours since he had gone off. He told them he had located the thieves and the stolen animals. The commander did not believe him and accused him of having taken three hours to goof off in the dunes, perhaps taking a nap. After all, no one could have tracked anything through this sand.

He chose seven backup men and led them to the spot. The thieves were arrested, the animals returned.

One day an entire flock of 600 sheep disappeared from a kibbutz. It was the entire capital stock of the kibbutzniks and they would be bankrupt if the flock were not recovered. The Scout followed their tracks and found the animals grazing in a desert gully. He shook his police cap to get their attention and the entire flock followed him home, like Little Bo Peep. The press was on hand to photograph the grand entrance and the party thereafter.

The kibbutz offered him four of the choice sheep as reward. He refused.

*   *   *   *

One day he got a panicky call to report to a large army base. The razor wire around the base had been cut in three places. The entire base was on alert. They feared infiltrators were inside, preparing some sort of attack.

He searched the area near the break-in points and saw that the footprints were of girls. He then noticed some civilian girls chatting on the public phones in the base. There are your infiltrators, he said. The soldiers had been smuggling their girlfriends into the camp.

*   *   *   *

The head of state in Israelis is the Prime Minister, but there is also a President, largely an honorary position, who represents the country at state affairs and formally. One day in 1954, the President showed up in Ashkelon, where he had leased a vacation home near the beaches. He was accompanied in his car by his wife, a driver and General Moshe Dayan, the famous military hero with the black patch over one eye.

Salim was assigned to accompany them and show them around the area. At one point the tire of the Landrover exploded, and they all got down in the dust to change it. We have a "bencher," the Scout explained. The President's wife did not comprehend. He pointed at the flat tire. You mean puncture, she said. Exactly, bencher. Arabic has no "P" sound. As the others turned the bolts, she sat at the side of the road and tried to teach him to say "puncture." They could not control their laughter. Puncture, bencher, puncture, bencher.

When they returned to the presidential vacation home, they discovered a new problem. The line on the flagpole on the roof had torn and fallen down. It was unthinkable that the President stay there without the flag raised above the house. No problem, the Scout said. He took off his boots and climbed the pole barefoot, planting the flag aloft. Moshe Dayan had grown up with Bedouins near his farm cooperative in the Jezreel Valley. "Yep," said the general as Salim climbed back down the pole, "now *that* is a Bedouin!"

* * * *

ix. The Oleanders

THE SUN WAS RISING over Camp Cesspool, a large Israeli army base. I was waiting for a Munchkin to relieve me from guard duty. It had been a cold, quiet night. It was supposed to rain later.

Cesspool was the filthiest army base I had ever seen, on either side of the Green Line, the border separating Israel from the occupied territories. It is an urban base, located within a city. In a sense this made things all the more frustrating, knowing that civilization, clean sheets and decent food were all just a few meters away on the other side of the barbed wire perimeter. 'Twas a time when Cesspool was the model military base, with spick and span facilities, spotless mess halls, and a Head to inspire pride in the heart of all soldiers. But when the commandant was changed a few years earlier, everything fell apart and degenerated into its current state of filth.

Anyone suspecting that Israelis are militarists has never observed the despair and outrage of someone receiving a reserve order to report for active duty. No Brooklyn longshoreman could produce similar expletives.

Reserve duty is based upon a reversal of the quantum principle, proving that in fact time slows down when the speed of a body approaches zero. It has also been described as an inversion of Descartes: I do *not* think, therefore I am a reservist.

The stench of gun grease is the first part of the initiation into a reserve tour of duty. At the armory I ask for my equipment, addressing the soldier on duty with politeness to which he is unaccustomed. "How come you are speaking 'Old'?" he asks me. One signs for the rifle, coated with grease, which gets into one's hair, clothes, fingers. It stays with one even after showering, like a bad memory. For weeks, everything tastes and smells of it. The food in Cesspool is so awful that the gun grease is somewhat of an improvement. The Munchkins do not complain about it.

The Munchkins are a strange group of regular soldiers, *Sadirniks*, aged 19–20. They are the anomalies of the Jewish state, the forgotten slow ones, the exceptions to the stereotype of Jews being great scholars and intellectuals and academics in high-tech Israel. The Munchkins are all D students, dropouts, borderline literate. They are just at the cut-off, the bottom minimal standard for what the army will accept as soldier material. A few IQ points less and they'd be classified as learning disabled and never conscripted, condemned to joblessness and failure in life. For them, the army is their last, best chance. They will emerge eventually with an honorable discharge, a passport into employment and blue-collar opportunity in the Israel of the 21st century.

They are a mixed batch, about half from Russia and Georgia (the one in the Caucasus mountains), the rest native-born sabra Israelis. Even the army understands that they cannot be made into mechanics and technicians, let alone officers or operators of high-tech military equipment. They do endless guard duty, the one and only task they appear capable of performing. For them, it is a sort of preparation for life. They are ordered about, fulfill instructions as well as they can.

I lucked out when I became one of the reservists called up to supplement the Munchkins in guarding Cesspool. Yanked out of my classroom, away from research and data crunching to play soldier. The Munchkins crowd about, staring at my ruby slippers (beat-up smelly army boots) in awe. They have never met a university professor before. I am nicknamed "The Professor" by a Munchkin I name Gilligan, but he has never seen the show.

The Munchkins sleep on and off during the days, guard most of the night, seemingly used to this regimen. A four-hour guard detail of inactivity drives me to the brink of insanity, but the Munchkins take it in stride, and sometimes even hang out for a while after being relieved, just to chat.

Reservists take a less literal attitude towards military orders and officers than do regular soldiers. We are all under orders to sleep with

our army boots on, as Cesspool is in a state of permanent alert. When
pigs are kosher, I chuckle. But the Munchkins, I later observe, actually obey this order. They badmouth officers during briefings, out of
a sort of pathetic Munchkin bravado, and receive repeated petty pun-
ishments for it, but are obedient and well-behaved otherwise.

The Munchkins are really not a bad group, just slow. Alex, a Russian Munchkin, likes to hang out with me during his off-duty time
and ask questions. Did I leave America because the Mafia was trying
to kill me? Could I please explain to him how exactly he could get
rich? He asks me to read and translate for him the inscription by the
manufacturer on my M-16. He has gotten quite good at smuggling a
large old Russian radio into the guard post with him, and has never
been apprehended, so I am certain he has great potential for success
in later life.

Twice a day the Munchkins are assembled for their daily briefings,
and we reservists have to tag along. The briefings are pretty much the
same every day. The usual reminders of proper procedures, warnings
to be on the lookout for this or that, ammunition belts and weapons
checked. By the third day I can recite the briefing in my sleep. That is,
if I were getting any. As a reservist, I only have to listen to this for a
couple of weeks, and I am already going nuts from the repetition; the
Munchkins do not seem to mind, and indeed keep answering some
of the questions incorrectly, even though they have heard them asked
and answered over and over again for a year or more.

At night the briefing is followed by a fire drill. The Munchkins do
all the work, with the reservists passive, off to the side. The Munchkins have done the drill each night since they came to Cesspool. And
they still cannot get it right. They trip over one another, attach the
hoses incorrectly, spritz water all over one another. Sleeplessness is getting to me. Watching them, I am getting a flashback from the Disney
Dumbo movie, where the clowns with floppy long shoes come out
dressed as firemen, fall all over one another, and eventually spritz all
over Dumbo.

Reserve duty is about killing time, not killing people. I have
brought along some English books and bluegrass tapes, this choice –
to insure they will not be stolen. Most of the other reservists have

brought along cellular phones, and chat nonstop. One, Wassily, is the regiment clown and has everyone rolling in laughter. Another, Moti, is awaiting his first baby in a few weeks. To kill time, I run a private Lamaze course for him.

Everything in the army is an acronym. Like that Robin Williams routine where he makes an entire speech composed of military acronyms.

Since its moral decline into studied abandon, the greatest asset in Cesspool is having a key to one of the hidden private bathrooms. Like executives in a Madison Avenue office, you know when you have made it when you get your own washroom key. I have not made it. The private facilities are kept locked against all invaders. Including reservists.

The rest of the world, and this includes the reservists, must use the fearsome Head. A dismal grotto of a bathroom, caked with ancient filth. Where one dare not allow one's flesh to make contact with any stationary object. A scene out of Dante. Dark and gloomy. And it is here, of all places, where the mystery was revealed.

* * * *

Oleanders are a common decorative shrub used in Israel, just like in California and Florida. Pink and white flowers. No fragrance. Only one thing, though. They are poisonous. Lethally poisonous. Every last bit of them. The flowers, leaves, stems. Everything.

"Bootka" is a Russian word. One of many that have entered modern Hebrew. The Bootka is a small guardhouse, about 5 feet by 5 feet, and 7 feet high. More of a guardshack. Windows in all sides. Guards must man it 24 hours a day, seven days a week, 365 days a year. It strategically covers and provides fire backing for the gate guard, so that if an intruder were to force the gate, the guard in the Bootka would call him to order. With an M-16.

The Bootka is stiflingly hot during the day and freezing cold during the night. Guards therein are prohibited from listening to the radio while on guard duty, as it might cause them to remain awake. Yet I have fashioned a hidden line under the uniform and ammunition belt that connects to the hidden walkman, and Garth Brooks is keeping me warm. It is night and Mother Hen is asleep.

Mother Hen is the camp's Sergeant Major, in charge of making sure all army boots are shined. He does not care about the filth and the awful food and – having a blessed key of his own – I doubt he has ever entered the fearsome Head. He stops regular soldiers who walk by his office and makes them shine their boots. It is his calling in life and he takes his sacred mission seriously. He knows better than to order reservists to shine their boots, and mine have not seen shinola since the Reagan Administration. Mother Hen has only addressed himself to me once. I am wearing a Senegalese army sun cap, one I picked up for pennies in a Berkeley secondhand shop, probably left over from the sixties and the Diggers. You are out of uniform, snarls the Hen, why are you not wearing an army cap? This is an army cap, I insist, just not the Israeli army's. Mother walks away shaking his head in disbelief.

A Brigadier General has driven into Cesspool and asks me if it is ok if he parks near the Bootka in which I am ensconced. Sure, I reply, would you like the car waxed? He chuckles. He walks off and, dear God, he has entered the Head. Was he not warned? Will he ever be heard from again?

*   *   *   *

A book of short stories was published recently in Israel. By one Leah Aini. It is called Oleanders. It is a collection of bizarre love stories. One story in the book Oleanders is itself called Oleanders. It is about (I am not making this up) a woman student at the university in the economics department and an officer in the military who serves in Camp Cesspool.

On one of my first evenings in the Bootka, a lieutenant has come by and struck up a conversation. He is as amazed to find a college teacher in the Bootka as I am to be in it. We get to talking. He tells me that his girlfriend is doing a seminar paper in Beer Sheba in econometrics and she is stuck, unable to resolve a data problem for weeks now. Tell me all about it, I insist, I have nowhere to go. Ten minutes later the problem is resolved.

Next night, his friend, a young captain, comes by. He is doing an MBA and wanted to ask a few questions in finance. When we finish,

I ask him to pass on my regards to his Dean. But who should I say is sending regards, he asks. Just tell him the Private from the Bootka. How come a college professor is doing this awful job, he asks. Well, all the generals' slots were taken, I explain.

Word has gotten out among Cesspool's officer corps that technical help is available for students at the Bootka. Many of the officers are part-time students. They come by with questions about business courses, economics problems, the internet, even mortgage shopping. I feel like Lucy in the old Peanuts comic strip, sitting at her booth with the sign offering psychiatric advice for 25 cents a pop. I am considering dispensing numbers for service at the beginning of each watch. I offer the officers a deal: get me off a watch or two and I will come give the whole officer's barracks a talk on MBA studies. A major walks by the Bootka, and sees the group of officers lining up, including one colonel, standing outside the Bootka, trying to figure out who the important military personality is inside whom everyone is tring to see, but only sees a middle-aged private. What was the name of the private in Catch 22 who ran the whole army?

Toilet paper theft is a major problem at Cesspool. It is in a state of perpetual scarcity, and the soldiers steal from one another. The ingenuity they display is what allows the Israeli army to win wars. I have come equipped with a lock and keep my private stock well secured, except for ventures into the Head.

At lunch I join some Munchkins. I demand an investigation, I tell them, the bread today is fresh, which means that the kitchen staff has neglected to carry out its sworn duty and store it until hard and stale. The Munchkins are not sure if I am serious or joking.

Alex comes by the Bootka, and peels some oranges with the sharp tip of a bullet. He has gotten grounded, denied leave for two weeks, because he left his rifle behind in his barracks room when going for a walk and got caught. One is expected to have it on one at all times. Even in the Head.

On my hidden radio it is announced that the army has decided that college students will not be called up for more than 21 days of reserve duty this year. As for professors, apparently the limit does not apply.

Moti has developed a skin infection, and the cream the army medic gave him is not working. Have you been going into the Head without your Space Walk uniform, I ask. I am a walking pharmacy, having learned in past reserve stints to bring along creams for every conceivable skin affliction known to mankind. I fix him up and within days he is back to normal.

*   *   *   *

It is 4:00 in the morning. Shivering in the Bootka. I ask some Munchkins on the patrol to take over for me for a bit to allow me to visit the Head. I stumble in. The fumes and filth attack every sensory organ.

And suddenly, there it is. The grand mystery. Cesspool's answer to Stonehenge. Looking up, for the first time – it must be – since coming to Cesspool. White lights seem to be flashing. I try to make sense of it.

On the walls of the booth, staring out at me, someone has composed a lyric poem and written it here in careful letters. It is entitled Oleanders. It covers the whole stall. It is lovely, although loses everything in translation. Here in this God-forsaken place, amid the stench and the squalor, the bowels of Camp Cesspool, someone has decorated the wall with a poem. A work of indescribable beauty.

Who put it there? Surely it was not the Munchkins. Mother Hen would never have thought of it. The officers never come in here. Was it to be a joke? A protest? An act of desperation?

x. The Tracks

WHAT HAD BEGUN as a routine police position, tracking common thieves, was being transformed into a job spent more and more in hunting down terrorists and murderers. One night he was called to a kibbutz not far from the Gaza Strip. There were signs of a break-in. In the fields nearby the Scout found the place where the infiltrator had spent several hours the night before, before cutting through the kibbutz perimeter. Fortunately, something had scared him off before he could do anything violent.

One night at 10:00 o'clock the police station siren was sounded. Near Ashkelon two brothers had been delivering milk bottles from their horse and wagon. They had been brutally murdered. The Scout was called in. It was pitch dark and it was dangerous to track at night; the quarry could be hiding anywhere, and there had been more than one case where the hunted had picked off the hunters with rifles.

The police slept in their police cars until daybreak. In the morning, the commander, named Max, showed up and ordered the bloodhounds home. They were not needed when the Scout was present.

The reins of the horse that had been pulling the milk cart had been cut and the horse stolen. The tracks pointed towards Gaza. The terrorists had cut through a wadi near the border laced with land mines, but had managed to cross unscathed.

Near the Gaza border, which at the time was nothing but a plow furrow, some UN observers stopped them. They were informed of what had transpired and shown the tracks by the Scout. The prints of five people and a horse were clearly visible. But the UN personnel insisted they could see nothing to indicate the terrorists had passed that way. Then Egyptian police, riding camels, appeared and ordered the Israelis to retreat. The Egyptians forced the camels to kneel and took up positions behind them, with rifles aimed. The Israelis had to abandon the hunt.

* * * *

A Bedouin scout can distinguish between foot prints of a man and a woman, between those of old and young. He can tell what hour of day a person has left tracks, from the way he walked. He can tell from tracks if a woman is pregnant. Some say he can tell what sort of personality someone has from the tracks left. A person's foot prints are like fingerprints, the scouts insist. Different for everyone.

As a police scout, he dealt with every sort of trickery imaginable. There were those who tried to hide their footprints by covering their shoes with fleece and then walking backwards. There were those who attached poles and blocks to their shoes.

Such tricks were childish. An insult to his tracking skills.

* * * *

When the call arrived from Scorpion Pass, he was about to leave for the evening and head home on furlough. He had bundles of sweets and toys for his children. He handed them to the duty officer and ordered him to guard the treasures with his life.

When he arrived at Scorpion Pass, there was blood and horror everywhere. Other trackers had already gone over the scene, but had found nothing. When the commander saw him, he ordered the others to move out of the way. "The *Kimawi* has arrived," he announced. "*Kimawi*" is a corruption of "chemist" in Arabic. The Scout was considered to be a walking forensics laboratory.

He picked up the trail of the killers. He found a satin hat nearby, one with an embroidered white "eye" above the brim, a common good-luck symbol among Jordanian Arabs.

The massacre was already getting international attention and the government was taking enormous heat to identify the source of the attack. Because of the political sensitivity, a Swedish United Nations observer was assigned to accompany the tracking team. The Swede was a pompous fool. He decided to hike part of the way barefoot,

Bedouin-style, and before long his feet were leaving spattered stains of blood on the ground.

They tracked until nightfall. Their water was getting low. An army command car found them and dropped off supplies.

The next day at dawn the hunt resumed. The ground was very hard and the UN observer could see nothing to indicate that the murderers had passed this way. The Scout ignored him. He followed the trail until it reached the Jordanian border.

The Prime Minister had his answer. The murderers had infiltrated from Jordan.

*   *   *   *

At the border, a Jordanian officer challenged them. The murderers from Scorpion Pass have passed this way, they explained. Nonsense, insisted the Jordanian. Bring your own scouts here, Salim suggested. The officer called in some Jordanian army scouts. They examined the signs. He is right, they confirmed. These are the tracks.

*   *   *   *

The resolution of the massacre was followed by Israeli reprisal raids into Jordanian territory. The main strike was on the West Bank town of Nahhalim, which had been a frequent jumping-off site for terrorist raids into Israel. The attack was code named Operation Lion, and was led by Ariel Sharon, who would later save his country from destruction during the 1973 Yom Kippur War and much later become Israeli Prime Minister. The raid was widely seen as retaliation for the Scorpion Pass massacre. Other reprisal raids followed, on places with names like Zeita, Khirbet Jinba, Deir al-Ghusun, Falama, and 'Azzun. The country breathed easier. The government had weathered its political crisis.

But the violence did not cease. Terrorist infiltration continued from both Jordan and Egypt. He was regularly assigned to the investigation and tracking. Eventually the attacks would trigger the 1956 Arab-Israeli War, when the Israeli military struck at the *fedayeen* bases in the Sinai Desert and blasted its way to the Suez Canal.

*   *   *   *

A pretty young nurse named Marina from somewhere in the Ukraine is changing his bandages. She came to Israel after the Chernobyl disaster. She is making conversation, asking about what sort of work he did before retirement. He speaks freely about himself with her. I was a scout, he explains. Worked with the army and police. I was the one who tracked the killers in the Scorpion Pass massacre.

I am listening in with half an ear, slowly dozing off.

But suddenly I am jolted into full consciousness. The nurse just nods politely. She does not understand what he has just told her. She is new in the country, and probably has never heard of him.

It is he. The legend. The Scout. I have been lying next to him for nearly a week, sharing torment and indignity. Not knowing who he is.

*   *   *   *

It is related that in the days of the Caliph Muawiya, a Bedouin scout named Abdullah ibn Kulaba went out into the Arabian desert to search for a missing camel. After searching for many hours, he saw in the distance tall towers and a palace with enormous walls, dazzling as if made of gold. The gates of the city were open, decorated in gold and jewels, but there were no humans to be seen. The palace, also decorated with gold and precious stones, was deserted. But most astonishing was that in the center of the palace were huge gardens full of fruits and flowers of every color. The scout took a handful of diamonds and returned to the Caliph.

The Caliph then sent out a full expedition, led by the same Abdullah, to the site of the palace. But alas, when they arrived they found only empty desert.

*   *   *   *

One day a group of schoolchildren visited the police station. They asked in particular for the Scout to speak with them and to explain how trackers operate. The commander was apprehensive. But the Scout assured him the schoolchildren would have a memorable experience.

He lined up the 50 children in a row and then walked off, to a place from where he could not see them. While he was away, ten of the 50 took a few steps forward and then returned to the line. Their positions in the line were then shuffled.

He returned, studied the prints in the dirt in front of the row, then quickly and correctly identified from the tracks left the ten who had stepped forward.

* * * *

Since retiring from the security forces, he serves as a trainer of army and police scouts. He runs special courses. He continues to serve one day a week with the security forces and is called up for duty whenever the younger scouts are stumped and when his special talents are needed. He insists they do not make army scouts like they used to.

In recent years, northern Israel has been the scene of frequent forest fires. Many suspect they are acts of arson by terrorists, in effect environmental sabotage. The Scout is often called in for these cases. He quickly identifies which fires were accidental and which were arson.

* * * *

Sergeant Major Halil Taher was a Bedouin scout in the Israeli army when he was killed by a roadside bomb planted inside Israel by the Hizbollah terrorists in Lebanon in November 2000. It was a few months after Israel withdrew from its Security Zone in southern Lebanon and the area was turned over to the Iran-backed and Syrian-controlled Hizbollah. This was the withdrawal that was supposed to produce tranquility on Israel's northern border. Halil was from a family of scouts who had served in the Israeli military; four of his brothers served in the army before him.

After he was killed, his family, who live in Acre, were harassed by local Moslems, urged to do so by the *imam,* or Moslem religious leader of Acre. The *imam* officiates at the Mosque of al-Jazzar in the old Crusader town, and his salary is paid by the Israeli taxpayer. Local Moslems sent death threats to Halil's family, insulted them and shunned them during the days of mourning after his death. The officials at the Moslem cemetery refused to read passages from the

Holy Koran at his funeral. He had died as a military hero serving his country and for this reason his family was stigmatized in Acre.[13] He was 27 years old. He was married and had a newborn son.

*   *   *   *

---

13 Press source: *Haaretz*, December 1, 2000.

XI. The Rabbi

MEDIEVAL HAIFA MET a violent demise when the Crusader Franks were transported to the city in Venetian galleys, commanded by the Doge himself. An earlier wave of Crusaders had decided to bypass the fortified town altogether and to hurry onwards towards Jerusalem. But in 1100 Crusaders attacked Haifa from the land and from the sea. The Jewish and Moslem defenders in the town took to the walls and withstood weeks of ferocious bombardment.

The attackers were about to give up when 20 of the leading knights swore a sacred oath to infiltrate the city or die in the attempt. The defenders poured down boiling oil and tar upon them, but were slowly driven from the main defending tower. Finally, the knights broke into the city and opened the gates for the rest of the Crusader forces. Most of the inhabitants of Haifa were massacred in a frenzy of bloodshed.

A special poem was composed for the Jewish martyrs of Haifa, entitled "The Elders of The Circle." It referred to the Jewish sages of the city, whose days had been spent before the massacre in studying the sacred books in a circular threshing area. The poem was read in synagogues around the world.

*   *   *   *

The intravenous tube has been removed at last. I know it is supposed to contain all the nutrients one needs, like astronaut rations, but my stomach has been growling and filled with hunger pangs throughout the days of being fed via the tubes. And when I am at last detached, the hunger gets worse. The hospital food consists of disgusting pabulum, something that looks like what I fed my children in their first months of life. And to make things worse, the "dinner" is served at about five o'clock in the evening. So by eight, my hunger pangs are back.

It is as if the whole boarding system of the ward is designed to generate weight loss. Feed a cold and starve a cancer.

*   *   *   *

Following the ultimate defeat of the Crusaders, and for centuries thereafter, the town of Haifa lay in ruins, a backwater in the Mamluk and then the Ottoman empires. The port fell into disuse, as merchant ships feared the pirate enclaves in the hills near the town.

At the beginning of the eighteenth century, Dahar al-Amar was the most powerful Bedouin tribal chief of the Galilee. In 1730 he conquered the fortress of Acre and converted it into his capital. Al-Amar was involved in a long-running conflict with a number of Bedouin sheikhs on Mount Carmel. He invaded Haifa, which was still little more than a coastal colony, and destroyed its walls and defenses so that it would not be seized by his enemies and used against him. He later rebuilt the town further inland, partly up the slope of the mountain, protected by a new fortress named *Burj a-Salaam*, the fortress of peace.

The Ottomans regarded the sheikh as a rebel and renegade. In 1775, the Turkish legions put an end to his family's rule in Haifa. A new Turkish regime was introduced into Acre, led by a new *Pasha*, Ahmed Jazar. His financial advisor was a Jew from Damascus, one Haim Farhi. During their administration, Jewish immigrants trickled into Haifa, mainly from North Africa, renewing the Jewish community there.

*   *   *   *

He was one of the greatest of the Chassidic masters of Eastern European Jewry. His followers, known for their bouts of euphoric dancing and singing, are to be found throughout the world to this day. He was the great-grandson of the Baal Shem Tov, or Master of the Good Name, who had founded Chassidism, the movement of Jewish mysticism that was embraced by much of European Jewry in the 17th century.

Born in the Ukraine, the young Rabbi Nahman of Breslov was a revered scholar and teacher in his own right when he one day announced that he had decided to make the treacherous journey to the Holy Land. "Wherever I walk," he was renowned for saying, "I am in fact going to the Land of Israel." He would go as a sort of scout on behalf of all Jews. And besides, the studying of the Holy Books in the Holy Land was like no other form of study; it was a surefire guarantee of entrance into the World to Come.

Nearly penniless himself, the great Rabbi left his family behind, convinced that God and his followers would provide for them. He and an attendant booked boat passage to Odessa on the Black Sea and from there somehow reached Istanbul. He kept his identity secret from the Jews of the city, taking on a new pseudonym each day. The year was 1798. The Sultan was at war with the French, who had invaded his territories in Egypt, and his officials saw French spies behind every alien face. The Istanbul Jewish merchants feared venturing to the Holy Land, lest they fall into the hands of Napoleon's troops, driving quickly from Egypt and through Palestine.

Somehow, the Rabbi found a ship that was transporting pilgrims to the Holy Land. When they approached the spot traditionally regarded as the location in which the Prophet Jonah had been thrown into the sea, a violent storm suddenly broke. The Rabbi convinced all on board that if they would sit in perfect silence, the storm would pass. They did, and it did.

Finally they reached the port of Jaffa. Turkish officials in Jaffa came on board to check the crew and the cargo and to accept the usual *baksheesh* bribes. When they saw the Rabbi with his long side curls, part of the standard dress of Eastern European Jews, they were convinced he must be a French spy, for why else would anyone dress so oddly. They refused to let him disembark.

Instead, the ship took him back up the coast and left him off in Haifa. It was the day before Rosh Hashana, the Jewish New Year, when shofar rams' horns are sounded like trumpets and the very fate of the world is in balance. The Rabbi went to the cave of the Prophet Elijah, then to the ritual bathhouse, and spent the holidays with the local Jews.

One day a young Turk came to the lodge in which the Rabbi was staying in Haifa. He conducted a very long conversation with the Rabbi in Turkish, a language of which the Rabbi did not speak a single word. The Turk then returned again and again, day after day, with the same long colloquy in Turkish.

One day, the Turk appeared as usual, but in a different mood. He was full of rage, and screamed at the Rabbi. A woman from Romania who understood Turkish explained that the Turk had just challenged the Rabbi to a duel!

The next day, the Turk returned, but mysteriously had resumed his earlier tone of deference and friendship for the Rabbi. He even offered the Rabbi a team of mules to take him on a pilgrimage to Tiberias.

The Jews of Haifa were astounded. What was going on between the Rabbi and the Turk? In time the Rabbi would explain. He claimed the Turk was in fact none other than the Evil One, the Destroyer himself. God had intervened, had rescued him and protected him.

* * * *

The nurses are civil and helpful, all except for one. She is a huge Russian with a mean streak and an attitude. She has imported with her a Soviet-era bedside manner. She waddles down the hall and bad-mouths everyone, although I actually get her to crack a smile once. The patients are afraid of her. One calls her Eva Braun.

She especially has it in for Benno. He is an irritating Romanian Jew, who never stops complaining about trivial things. He has been trying the patience of all the patients in the ward, who pretend to be dozing whenever he comes near to chat. He makes the mistake of complaining to her about something or other and the ward is suddenly tensely silent, all focused on nothing but the emerging confrontation. She gives him the tongue lashing of his life and he runs off with his catheter bag, like a dog's tail, between his legs.

There are no televisions about, and nothing beats live entertainment.

*   *   *   *

In the very days when Rabbi Nahman was in Haifa, the war was drawing near. Napoleon's army was approaching the city in its march to Acre. The Rabbi took his entourage of followers and headed for Tiberias until the fighting should pass. In Tiberias he spent his days meeting with the sages of the town and visiting the grave shrines of the famous Rabbis of the Talmud. His own grandfather, the great sage Rabbi Nahman Horodenker, was buried there.

Suddenly the Rabbi decided that he must immediately return to Europe. He offered no explanation. He managed to reach the port of Acre, but faced a new problem. Napoleon's troops were approaching and the 15,000 Turkish soldiers inside Acre were expecting the battle to commence within two days. The only ships in the harbor besides the British warships stalking Napoleon were Turkish merchant ships, but anyone venturing on board these was in danger of being impressed. Meanwhile the Pasha had ordered all civilians to abandon the city of Acre at once, to allow his troops better maneuvering room within the city.

*   *   *   *

The walled city of Acre in 1799. Crowds of panicky people of many races moving in all directions. Children screaming. In the confusion, the attendant could not find the Rabbi. A woman at the lodge announced that she had seen him heading towards the waterfront. But he had left his chests and belongings behind. His attendant and some other followers carried the bags to the dock, passing along below the fortress walls atop which Turkish troops were awaiting the French assault.

At last the attendant saw a small Turkish fishing boat with a single sail. Calmly sitting aboard its deck was the great Rabbi. The attendant got himself rowed out and joined the Rabbi with their gear. The fishing boat left the port and carried them down the coast to

Haifa, now well behind the battlefront. They hopped aboard the first large vessel they could find, but to their surprise it turned out to be a Turkish Man-of-War, bristling with cannon barrels. By going aboard they had unexpectedly allowed themselves to be conscripted into the Ottoman war against Napoleon.

They could not understand a single word of the Turks. The captain of the warship offered the Rabbi a private cabin room. The Rabbi's attendant was handed a musket and ordered to deck. The ship sailed back toward Acre and entered the battle against the French. Cannon balls were flying about

Suddenly a man entered their cabin and spoke to them in Russian. Don't you fools realize you are in the middle of a battle? Leave at once! They gathered their belongings and tried to find a way off of the ship and back to shore. But they needed the Russian-speaking stranger to help them communicate. They searched the entire ship but there was no Russian to be found and no one on board had ever heard of such a person.

The Rabbi and his attendant had boarded with no food or even water. But the ship's cook took pity on them and gave them provisions.

* * * *

The battle was over. Napoleon had been defeated. The Turkish warship with the Rabbi was now on the open seas. He had no idea where it was taking him.

A few days later they suddenly felt the ship dock. They asked the cook where they were. "The land of Adal," he replied. Adal was rumored to a place where Jews were immediately killed as human sacrifices. But before the natives could board the ship, a sudden storm tore the ship away from the dock, snapping its lines, and blew the ship back out to sea.

For days the storm raged. The ship was being slowly flooded and the efforts at pumping out the water from inside were failing. Water was flooding in faster than it could be pumped out. The ship seemed doomed. A passing ship of Greeks broke up in the storm and its passengers drowned.

The Rabbi ordered his attendant to take each of the coins they were carrying with them and to break them in two. He ordered the attendant to bind one set of halves to his body while the Rabbi took the other set. "Why bother," asked the attendant, "The fish can swallow us just as easily without the coins." "Do as I tell you," said the Rabbi. "Those crossing through the parted Red Sea did not fear, and we have even less reason for despair. After all, we are still inside of a ship."

Off the starboard suddenly a waterspout appeared. A tornado over water. It was approaching the ship. But miraculously, just as the ship was about to be sucked into the vortex, the clouds parted and the ship passed through unharmed. At the same time, the sailors discovered where the leak in the hull was located. They slaughtered a ram on board and used its skin to plug the leak. The ship was almost out of provisions, but reached a deserted rock of an island, covered with carob trees. They replenished the ship's stores with carobs and set off again.

It was the evening before Passover when they spotted land. It turned out to be the island of Rhodes, off the Turkish coast, once the home of the Crusader Hospitaler Knights, now an island of many Greeks with a thriving Jewish community. Some local officials demanded that the captain turn the famed Rabbi over to be held for ransom. The captain refused. His ship had been rescued through a miracle and he was not going to betray the Rabbi whose presence on board might just have produced that miracle. The Jews of Rhodes raised the 200 thalers needed to pay off the local officials to ensure the Rabbi's freedom, refusing to allow the Rabbi to use his own funds.

The central ritual of Passover is the Telling of the story. Every Jew is commanded by God to tell the story of "his" rescue from slavery in Egypt, as if he personally had taken part in the biblical Exodus. It is the entire point of the Passover Seder. More generally, when a Jew is beneficiary of a miracle, or when Jews are collectively so, telling about it is a religious obligation. On that Passover, the Rabbi told not only the traditional story of the miraculous rescue of the Children of Israel from Pharaoh, but also of his own personal rescue aboard the Turkish gunship.

Eventually the Rabbi returned to the Ukraine, establishing his court in Breslov and later in Uman, where he died at the age of 38. When the same Napoleon he had faced in Acre conquered Moscow, he was teaching and studying quietly.

He often taught that while he had been in the Holy Land, he had learned that one must develop longing and yearning for the closeness of God as if one had never ever before approached Him or tried to serve Him. The same way one who had committed every imaginable transgression would beg for forgiveness. In every hour and every day.

But at other times he would insist that he knew absolutely nothing at all, and had never learned anything at all.

*   *   *   *

As Napoleon fled from the coast of Acre in 1799 to return to France and to greater victories and defeats, his movements were being tracked by a British warship, commanded by one of Admiral Nelson's commanders, Cooper-Williams. The commander visited Haifa and in his diary described its residents as the most miserable he had ever seen anywhere in the civilized world.

It was the beginning of renewed European interest in the city. Little was left from Napoleon's invasion of the Levant, besides the obelisk in Concord Square and other artifacts carried to Paris, today to be seen in the Louvre.

In 1821, the Greeks revolted against the Turks, and the Greek homeland achieved independence. The Greeks in Anatolia and elsewhere however were violently suppressed. The Turks feared uprisings by Christians throughout their lands in support of the Greeks, and destroyed some of the Carmelite monasteries atop Mount Carmel, believing the monks were acting as spies on behalf of the rebels.

Starting in the nineteenth and continuing into the early twentieth century, Haifa developed a new role. It became a place of refuge for persecuted and exotic religious minority movements from the Moslem world.

True, Islam generally had a fairly good track record of toleration towards religious minorities, at least when compared with Europe.

Indeed, the Ottoman Empire, while hardly a paradigm of liberal democracy, was particularly tolerant of religious deviance. It was one of the main destinations for the Spanish Jews expelled from the Iberian peninsula after the Inquisition and Reconquista. But the line of Islam's moderation was drawn at the borders of monotheism. Those faiths regarded as *not* strictly worshipping a single Deity were beyond the pale. And special wrath was reserved for any group of Moslems who converted away from Islam or initiated what were considered heretical new faiths.

One such religious movement was launched in Lahore in what is now Pakistan in 1889. Its leader was Mirza Ghulam Ahmad and it is still referred to as the *Ahmadiyya*, named after him. While he and his followers regarded themselves as Moslems, and indeed as purifying reformers in their midst, they were rejected by the Moslem mainstream. Curiously, much of the theological conflict with the movement had to do with its views on the role of Jesus in Islam and suggestions by the founder that he himself was the reincarnated Jesus.

The *Ahmadiyya* were persecuted throughout the Moslem world and with special ferociousness on the Indian subcontinent. The internet today is filled with anti-Ahmadi hate sites set up by fundamentalists. Nevertheless, the movement sent out missionaries, attempting to attract both Moslems and Christians to their faith.

In 1928, a group of Arabs living on one of the slopes of Mount Carmel decided to join the *Ahmadiyya*, under the influence of a missionary from India. The community today maintains close ties with Ahmadis on all continents of the globe. The Ahmadi Mosque sits just across the wadi from our home. We hear the chant of the muezzin each evening as he calls his flock to prayer.

In 1844, a new religion was proclaimed by a 25-year-old man in Shiraz, Persia. Born Siyyid 'Ali-Muhammed, he called himself the *Bab* (or Portal to God), and claimed his purpose was to prepare mankind for the advent of a new revelation from God, one independent of Islam. His faith would be an eclectic one, drawing on theological lines from all of the world's major religions. It did not take long for the

Shi'ite clergy in Iran to declare him a heretic and have him arrested and imprisoned. In 1850 he was marched to the public square and executed by a firing squad.

But in the meantime his message had produced a flock of followers. The Iranian clergy went after these with special fury and 20,000 were executed throughout Persia following the death of the *Bab*. But others survived. Some managed to smuggle his earthly remains out of Persia and move them to Palestine. They were interred on the slopes of Mount Carmel, above the Templar colony.

The main apostle of the word of the *Bab* was an Iranian patrician named Baha'u'llah, whose name means the Glory of God. He claimed to trace his ancestry back to the Sassanid Emperors of pre-Moslem Persia. He too was imprisoned for repeating the heresy, in a Teheran dungeon known as the Black Pit. He wore a 100-pound iron prison chain around his neck, but he continued his mission. He was banished to Kurdistan and from there he traveled and preached in Baghdad, Istanbul and Adrianople. Finally, he was arrested by the Ottomans and sent to the Acre prison, the same building in which the British would later imprison the leaders of the Jewish underground in the dying days of the British Empire.

He continued to send out his epistles and the faith spread. His message was the imminent unification of humanity and the need for kings and rulers to put aside their differences and end war. The new faith became known as Bahai and today has followers in all corners of the globe.

When he died, Baha'u'llah was buried in Acre, not far from Napoleon's Hill. Meanwhile, Bahai devotees built a shrine with a golden dome over the tomb of the *Bab* on Mount Carmel. It is not only the main pilgrimage site for Bahais from around the world but also the most familiar symbol of Haifa, a beacon seen from ships far off as they approach the port of the Holy Land. It is surrounded by some of the most lush gardens in the Middle East, said to be a reproduction of the Hanging Gardens of Babylon, one of the Seven Wonders of the Ancient World.

*　*　*　*

It was more than a thousand years before the birth of Mohammed when Jews first settled in Iraq. It was 2500 years before the birth of Saddam Hussein. Of course it was called Babylon back then. The numbers of Jews there expanded during the era of Persian power. Most had arrived there when exiled from Jerusalem after the Temple of God had been destroyed by the Babylonians and the Land of Israel had been conquered. Then the Babylonians themselves were conquered by Persia, itself soon to fall before the armies of Alexander the Great.

More than 500 years before the birth of Jesus, the Persian King Darius was anxious to strengthen the loyalty of his frontier lands so that he could pursue his campaigns of conquest against Greece, campaigns that ended for him on the bloody plains of Marathon. He issued an imperial ruling: the Jews were to be allowed to return and rebuild Jerusalem. Many however stayed in place in the Iraqi Diaspora. Their fortunes waxed and waned. Iraq was a melting pot of Persians, Greeks, Armenians, Mazdeans and other cultures, with the Jews always in the midst of things. Here it was that Queen Esther saved the Jews from annihilation with her wit and charm.

For the next thousand years, the Jews of Iraq formed the religious, spiritual and literary center of world Judaism. The Iraqi Jews wrote and redacted the Talmud. They were the critical players in the preparation of Judaism for millenia of survival without a homeland and without a Temple.

A thousand years after Darius, the first Arab battalions stormed into the country, bringing the message of Islam, and driving out the pagan cults. The Iraqi Jews welcomed the Arab conquerors as liberators, as fellow children of Abraham, as Semitic cousins.

In time, Baghdad – *Balad al-Rashid* or the City of Rashid – became the seat of the Caliphate, the capital of the Arab world and the center of civilization, located near the ancient site of Babylon. Iraq remained the spiritual capital of the Jews until replaced by the emerging newer Arab-Jewish center in Spain after the scouting mission of Tarif.

* * * *

In the early 1940s, an Iraqi Jew named David Kazazz left for Beirut to study medicine there at the American University. Iraq was a dangerous place in those days. Plots galore to drive out the British governors and to ally local Arab nationalists with the Nazi Germans. Anti-Jewish pogroms. Xenophobia was in the air of Baghdad. The sort that would later give rise to – among other things – the dictator and butcher Saddam Hussein.

During a break from his schedule of classes in the 1940s, Kazazz hopped a Lebanese taxi going south into Palestine, together with some friends from med school. The border was open and beckoning in those days. The distance was such that they left Beirut before dawn and were on Mount Carmel by early morning. The taxi left them off in downtown Haifa, a metropolis of over 100,000 people. They wandered the streets and shops, and tried to speak Hebrew to the locals, who were almost all from Europe. Their alien Iraqi pronunciation, that spoken by Iraqi Jews without interruption for 25 centuries, was difficult for the locals to comprehend.

After Haifa, they spent some time in Tel Aviv. Kazazz got a temporary job there as a medical assistant in a hospital, a job conditioned on his never attempting to speak to The Professor, the medical demigod of the ward, even while tagging along behind him during rounds. Such things were just not done.

One day Kazazz was called to the treatment room. A young Bedouin youth was being treated there and he spoke no Hebrew. Kazazz spoke to him in Arabic. The youth's face brightened. Thanks to Allah, he sighed, you are an Arab doctor! Kazazz did not point out the error.

He had been friendly with Bedouin families back in Baghdad. His own father had adopted a Bedouin family whose father had died and had no sustenance. Kazazz' father had bought two milk cows and made a business deal with the orphan son, M'tayer. You take care of the cows. Provide us with a pitcher of milk daily except on the Sabbath, and you may sell the rest of the milk and use the proceeds to build up a business. Within months the orphan had his own dairy business with five cows and a wife who was the daughter of a sheikh.

But the Bedouin youth in the hospital ward was near hysteria. He insisted his medicine was coming out of his nose. The nurses had told him he must insert it, but it kept sliding out of his body.

It took a few minutes for Kazazz to make sense of things. The Bedouin had been given medical suppositories. But he had never heard of such things and the nurses were too embarrassed to spell out for him graphically how they must be used. He had tried to insert them in his nose.

Years later, Kazazz moved to Denver, Colorado, and worked as a psychiatrist. He set up an institute for documenting the history of the Jews of the Spanish Tradition. He wrote a book of memoirs entitled "Mother of the Pound,"[14] documenting the history of his family and of Iraqi Jews. The title is based on the story of how his sweetheart, now his wife, had defied the orders of the Iraqi regime prohibiting Jews from taking any money out of the country with them when they emigrated. She had a brooch made out of a British pound and wore it proudly as she boarded the plane taking her away from the land of her birth.

Kazazz had a cousin in Baghdad, an unusual young woman. In a city of dark Semitic faces, she had an exotic Aryan appearance, blue eyes and blond hair. Her father was official court physician, a position Jews commonly held in Moslem regimes. She too wanted to go to Beirut to study medicine, but such things were out of the question for a single woman, who should never venture outside without chaperone.

After Israel was created, she and almost all other Iraqi Jews were pressured into leaving Iraq under threat of violence, leaving behind all of their property. Despite having grown up in aristocratic wealth, she suddenly found herself in a refugee camp, full of tents and shanties and mud and despair, not far from Haifa in the new Jewish state. Her mother tongue was Arabic. A local Bedouin sheikh visiting the camp asked friends to find out if the Arabic-speaking German woman would agree to be his wife.

She took Hebrew classes, and married her Hebrew teacher, the

---

14 Sepher-Hermon Press, Inc., Brooklyn, 1999.

son of the Chief Rabbi of Haifa, a descendant of Rabbi Suleiman of Fez. The first daughter of the blond Iraqi cousin of Kazazz was born soon afterwards. She grew up to become my wife.

XII. The Benediction

Happy is the man whom You torment and chastise, Oh God.

– The 94th Psalm

THE WORD "CARMEL" means the vineyard or orchard of God. Mount Carmel is a natural spice garden. Along its slopes one finds growing naturally parsley, sage, rosemary and thyme, no joking. One of the symbols of Mount Carmel is the spice hyssop, or *zaatar* as it is called by both Jews and Arabs, a spice that grows wild on the mountain and in few other places. The university campus has lots of it. Its small leaves have a powerful aroma and unique taste.

In the Bible hyssop is part of the cocktail prepared by the priests of the Temple to cure leprosy. It is also a protection against death. In the story of the Exodus, God has set loose the Destroyer to kill all of the first-born in Egypt, from the first-born son of Pharaoh himself on down to the firstborn of the Egyptian farm animals. The Israelites are instructed to protect their homes by mixing the hyssop with the blood of a lamb and spreading the mixture on the doorposts. (Every Jewish firstborn son ever after is regarded as being specially indebted for having been spared. I am the firstborn in my family.) The Destroyer then passes over the Israelite homes in Egypt, and hence the name of the holiday, Passover.

No mention of whether the hyssop helps with cancer though.

Until a few years ago, it only grew wild, and was on the endangered list due to excess picking from the mountain slopes by aficionados. Then some Israeli horticulturalists figured out a way to grow it in a commercial manner. The main manufacturer today is a farm and factory in what had been the Templar colony of Galilean Bethlehem, the Galilean "House of Bread."

*   *   *   *

It has been two hours since the nurses brought in the "breakfast" and my stomach is already growling. His wife appears and tells me she has brought me something. We had been talking about *zaatar* the day before while she was visiting. She pulls out a home-made zaatar pizza, a slab of home-baked pita bread dripping with olive oil and drenched in zaatar and sesame. The zaatar is from the Bethlehem manufacturing center. I almost bite her fingers off when I pounce on it with animal hunger. The olive grease gets all over the hospital sheets. I don't care.

*   *   *   *

"Purge me with hyssop and I shall be clean;
wash me and I will be whiter than snow."

– Psalms 51, 8

*   *   *   *

Naima, his wife, greets me as I emerge from the shower.

I have dreamed of washing my hair every moment since the surgery. My scalp is dry and itchy. It is five days now and I have worked up the courage. My wife helps me. We find a plastic chair on which I can sit beneath the shower head, covering the surgery wounds with layers of towels to keep them dry. I tilt back my head and the small shower room is transformed into a hair salon.

Arabic must be the only language in the world in which there is a greeting for emerging from the shower. There are wishes and greetings for many things in all languages, but this must be unique.

"Naima," she says and I have never so enjoyed a shampoo. I can already walk down to the end of the corridor where there is a small dining area, in which the hospital cuisine is served. I no longer have any tubes running into or out of me. I have also become more particular about what sorts of substances I am willing to consume from the hospital tray. The pabulum is definitely out.

"I leave tomorrow," I tell Laptop Man.

"Good," he says, "This is no place for a young man."

*　　*　　*　　*

One of the most commonly found expressions from the Bible appears in the 16th Psalm. "I have set God always before me." It is a simple phrase, but one that appears in almost every synagogue building, usually carved above the ark in which the sacred scrolls are held, the most holy part of the synagogue. While it is familiar to nearly every Jew, it is curious to note that the sentence immediately preceding it is virtually unknown: "I will bless God who has counseled me; in the night I am chastised through my kidneys." The biblical Hebrew word for chastise (*yisur*) is the same as that for torment, and the same as for instruct. You instruct someone by chastising them.

Kidneys show up in other unexpected places as well. In the 26th Psalm, "Examine me, God, and test me, inspect my heart and my kidneys." Kidneys are often mentioned in the Bible in combination with the heart, as the parts of the body in which the essence of man is to be found. Jeremiah writes, "I, the Lord, search the heart and test the kidneys, in order to award all men according to their ways and as fruit of their deeds."

*　　*　　*　　*

The Psalms are traditionally attributed to King David. In particular, the 30th Psalm is said to have been written by David after he recovered from a life-threatening illness. In it he writes, "I cried out to You and You healed me, You lifted me up from the pit. In the evening lying down in tears, but in the morning awakening with bliss. Your countenance had been hidden from me and I feared, but You turned my obituary into dance, You opened my sack of mourning."

Hope his hospital food was better than mine.

*　　*　　*　　*

In Jewish tradition there are three sets of people whose sins are automatically wiped clean, who begin the next stage of their lives with a blank slate, with no baggage from the past, with no spiritual debts or dues to pay. The first is any king, a bit of "realpolitik" on the part of the rabbis, who realized that rulers, especially in the darker of human ages, would be called upon to perform certain unsavory tasks out of political necessity and reason of state.

But the other two sets are simple ordinary people. Of these, the first are newlyweds, grooms and brides. From the point of view of spiritual accounting, they are granted an automatic fresh ledger page. All of their previous transgressions are removed with a sort of divine delete key. The second set consists of those who have been mortally ill, but manage to recover and stand on their feet again. Their ordeal is regarded as wiping their slate clean. They emerge as blameless as the newborn. Their suffering serves as their total atonement. They are free. They are unspoiled. They are pure, at least for the moment.

*   *   *   *

There is a benediction that a Jew says when his life has been spared, when he has been rescued from a life-threatening danger. It is said before a congregation, whose members act in effect as witnesses, notaries.

"Blessed are You, God, King of the universe, who bestows good things upon those who are guilty, and who has bestowed every good-ness upon me."

The word for guilty, "*hayavim*," can also be understood to mean those who are indebted, those who are lacking or underqualified, or those who are undeserving. It is, I suppose, a strange formulation. Here we have what is supposed to be a declaration of joy and relief, of thanksgiving, but for the "undeserving."

Beneficiaries of divine favors and miracles are in imminent dan-ger of hubris and self-indulgence. In expressing his thanks, the person reading the blessing is forced to concede his unworthiness. Any rescue or salvation has occurred *NOT* because of his own intrinsic worth and goodness, but in spite of his unworthiness and underqualification. All of which, I suppose, makes miracles all the more miraculous. The blessing is designed first and foremost to prevent people from letting good fortune go to their heads. To "prevent the urine from rising to one's brain", as modern Hebrew slang would put it.

*   *   *   *

When she was facing death, Queen Esther consulted her cousin Mordecai. It is prohibited to enter the King's Chamber without invitation, and the punishment for doing so is death. But if she does not do so, a Holocaust will befall her people. The Scroll of Esther describes how Mordecai tells her that it may well be for this very purpose she was chosen to become queen in the first place.

"We do not know why things happen to us," the Scout says to me softly. He is still very weak. "Perhaps we were brought to this hospital ward, perhaps we have experienced all these horrors, as part of a plan. Perhaps it was meant for us to meet here and to tell our stories."

*   *   *   *

"And let there be no longer unto the House of Israel any cancerous briar or tormenting thorn."

– Ezekiel 28, 24